A Guide to New England's Landscape

"A weekend in New England will be even more enjoyable after being appraised for its many facets by *A Guide to New England's Landscape* . . . The book is truly riveting for anyone with just a little more than a casual interest in New England." **— New England Living**

"An excellent book to purchase before going . . ."
— Asbury Park Press, NJ

"A little gem of a book — clearly written, easy to read guide to the quirks and shapes of New England . . . Well organized and of broad scope, valuable for anyone who lives in or visits New England. It offers a unique understanding of the region." **— The Morning Union, Springfield, MA**

"One of the great features of this book is the way Jorgensen has compiled specific details to help a reader enjoy the landscape. At the end of each subject there is a list of a dozen or so places where the characteristics explained may be viewed." **— The Evening News, Southbridge, MA**

"A basic book for understanding New England's physical form and natural landscape." **— American Urban Guidenotes**

"Both a textbook and a travel guide . . . A good mix of the science, history, and interesting natural phenomena of the New England area. The book promotes an ecological awareness of the area that can be appreciated by visitors and residents alike."
— The Travel Book: Guide to the Travel Guides

A Guide to New England's Landscape / by Neil Jorgensen

An East Woods Book

The Globe Pequot Press

Chester, Connecticut

About the Author

Neil Jorgensen, author of *Southern New England: A Sierra Club Naturalist's Guide,* is a former college professor holding degrees from Tufts, Columbia and Harvard. He is a member of the Royal Horticultural Society, the American Rhododendron Society and has written landscape and gardening articles for *The Boston Sunday Globe* and *The New York Times.*

Mr. Jorgensen lives with his family in Harvard, Massachusetts, where he heads Neil Jorgensen and Associates, Inc., a firm specializing in residential landscape design and environmental consultation.

First Edition/Seventh Printing

Contents

List of Illustrations

Photographs

Maps and Diagrams

Photo Credits

All charts and diagrams as well as the photographs in this book are the work of the author, with the following exceptions: S. W. Bailey, 151; Fred Larsen, 90, 130; State of Maine, 70; C. Nash, Barbara B. Paine, 55; Dick Smith, title pages, 12, 38–39, 88–89, 92, 94, 156–157, 159, 162; Harry R. Stevens, 33; Vermont Marble Company, 36; Bradford Washburn, 121.

Preface

New England's points of interest have probably been described more times than those of any other region of the country. Dozens of guidebooks direct the traveler to historic sites, resorts, museums, and festivals. Most of these books, however, devote considerably less space to the region's points of natural interest. Aside from descriptions of New England's scenic showplaces — Acadia National Park, Cape Cod National Seashore, and the White Mountain National Forest — the traveler interested in the natural features will usually find little information in the conventional tourist guides.

But merely listing the points of natural interest, while helpful, would be of limited value only. To appreciate the landscape one must understand it. To the trained eye of a geologist, a certain mound of glacial gravel, for example, might be full of significance and meaning; to the casual observer it is merely a gravel mound. In addition to listing points of interest, therefore, I have attempted to show why they are interesting and how they fit into the total picture of the region's landscape.

The intent of this book, then, is to strike a balance between a scientific text on the aspects of the landscape and the conventional organization of a guidebook. The book is divided into sections describing certain features of the landscape and explaining their evolution. At the end of most sections I have included places where good examples of the features described may be seen.

Of course, any book of this size, attempting to explain the scenery and list the points of natural interest in a region as large as New England will fall far short of completeness on both counts. The complexities of New England's geology and plant geography — the two major components of the natural landscape — would require a whole shelf-full of volumes far thicker than this one, as well as considerable professional knowledge, to be fully understood. Likewise, a really comprehensive listing of the points of geologic and botanic interest — if indeed it were possible to compile such a list — would be far too ponderous to be of much use to anyone. This book is offered only as a starting point.

For those readers whose interest is stimulated by this book, there is a bibliography at the end of most sections. In these lists I have included only recent and readily available publications. Most of these, in turn, have their own bibliographies that can carry the interested reader still further. Many of the books, reports, and pamphlets are published by state and private agencies and hence are not generally available in bookstores. In an appendix I have provided mailing addresses where these non-commercial publications may be ordered.

It is difficult to hide one's own particular interests when writing a book of this sort. Another writer covering the same territory might have produced a far different book. If my own interests seem to burst forth here and there, I only hope that the reader will find places in the framework I have presented where his own particular interests — whether they be mountain climbing, gardening, trout fishing, or merely sitting under a tree — might be nurtured.

In this age of increasing urbanization the rocks, the hills, the forests and meadowlands have become more and more foreign elements to many Americans. Reading this book, of course, will not bring people closer to the land, but it may help those whose eyes are already open to achieve a deeper awareness of the natural environment.

Lastly, I must acknowledge the help I have received from several people. I should like to thank three men, each an expert in his particular field, for reading portions of the manuscript and offering many valuable comments and criticisms: Marland P. Billings, Albion R. Hodgdon, and Arthur N. Strahler. Dr. Strahler's splendid book, *A Geologist Looks at Cape Cod*, was in many ways the model from which this book was written. In addition, I must thank two friends, also experts in their fields, for their assistance: Charles Heventhal for his advice on style and organization; and Meredith Jones whose darkroom wizardry appears in many of the illustrations. My editor, Gail Stewart, and her husband Reed — a geographer, as luck would have it — also made large contributions to the final draft. I should also like to thank Harold Meeks for his excellent suggestions for the second edition. My greatest debt, however, is to my wife, Sue, for her many suggestions, for turning cut and pasted, crossed out and rewritten rough drafts into a legible manuscript, and most of all, for her patience and encouragement.

Harvard, Massachusetts

Introduction

The photograph on the opposite page, a scene typical of the western part of New England, illustrates one way of viewing the region's landscape. The basic framework of the scene, a valley bounded by hills on either side, reflects the shape of the underlying bedrock surface. The hills are knobs and ridges of bedrock; the valley, a hollow in the bedrock surface.

The ups and downs of the bedrock, however, only partially explain the appearance of the land. The softened and rolling contours of the fields at middle distance result from a thick veneer of mantle rock — the soil and loose material that in most parts of the region forms the actual surface of the land. In New England practically all of the mantle rock is glacial debris, a mixture of rock particles of various sizes left by vast ice sheets that once covered the region.

Another glance at the photograph will show that the landscape does not end at the surface of the ground; the green layer of vegetation that covers nearly every square inch of the ground is also an integral part of the scenery. One has only to imagine the same scene as grassland or desert to realize the importance of the vegetation in creating a particular landscape. New England's natural vegetative cover is forest; there are few parts of the region where trees will not grow. The fields in the photograph, if left untilled for a few years, would soon return to woodland, as indeed is happening in one of the fields at the left.

These three facets of New England's landscape suggest the plan of the book. Part I discusses the bedrock foundations; Part II, the mantle of glacial debris that in most places forms the actual surface of the land; and Part III, the green layer of vegetation — mostly forest — that hides the face of the earth.

The Berkshire Hills, Cheshire, Massachusetts.

13

Part I
The Bedrock Foundation

If we dig a hole in some randomly chosen spot in New England the chances are excellent that we will reach solid rock within 20 feet of the surface. This solid layer, known as bedrock, forms the crust of the earth and, in most parts of the world, determines the shape of the landscape. In New England, almost all of the elevations over 200 feet are knobs and ridges of bedrock; likewise, most of the larger lakes and river valleys occur in scooped-out bedrock basins and channels. Only in the Cape Cod region does the bedrock layer lie buried so deeply beneath the surface that, except by its absence, it plays no part in the landscape. Elsewhere the bedrock is covered by a thin veneer — less than 20 feet thick — of gravel and soil. Across most of New England it is possible to find spots where the bedrock is not covered at all but lies exposed on the surface as ledge.

In Part I we shall examine New England's bedrock framework, both the ups and downs of its surface and the substance of some of the rocks themselves.

Granite quarry near Barre, Vermont.

The View from Mt. Monadnock

Mt. Monadnock is the highest of several isolated mountains scattered across southern New Hampshire and central Massachusetts. On a clear day the view from its barren summit is splendid. To the north and east it is possible to see a sizable part of New Hampshire; to the west lie the long ridges of Vermont's Green Mountains. To the south a sharp-eyed observer can see the entire length of Massachusetts from Boston's Prudential Tower to Mt. Greylock near the New York border.

It is this southern view that a geologist would probably find most interesting. Except for a few other isolated mountains that here and there rise above the land, the

view in this direction is that of an almost uniformly flat plain. Stretching off to the horizon is a landscape that appears to have little more relief than a prairie. But the southern New England landscape is not one of flat plainland; it is more or less hilly throughout. Even from the mountaintop it is possible to look down on definitely rolling terrain nearby. It is only at a distance that the land appears flat. What we perceive as a distant plain is really the blending together of the hilltops. Nearly all of the hills in any one area rise to about the same elevation and, except where broken by the higher isolated mountains, together these hilltops produce the flat horizon.

To understand this landscape of isolated mountains and even-topped hills, one must go back in time. Southern and central New England has not always been the

Mt. Monadnock, Jaffrey, New Hampshire. A typical example of the isolated mountains that rise above the New England Upland.

region of rather bland scenery that it is today. The rock record contained in the hills clearly indicates that there were times when tremendous forces from deep within the earth slowly folded the rocks of the crust like sheets of paper and broke them along huge fractures called *faults*. In addition, the bodies of granite that lend substance to many of the hills and mountains of the region were then masses of molten rock that welled upward into the crust from below. Those forces probably also pushed the crust skyward into massive mountain ranges whose craggy and glacier-scored peaks may well have rivaled the present-day Rockies or even the Himalayas.

But all of this happened long ago. Geologists using modern dating methods have determined that the last of several great mountain revolutions took place over 200 million years ago. Since that time New England's rocky crust has yielded remarkably little information about the landscape over those intervening years.

One thing is fairly certain, however. The slow but inexorable work of erosion has continued unabated for these millions of years. Mountains, like all other land features on this planet, suffer from its ravages. The forces of water, wind, and ice will in time destroy even the hardest of rock and could reduce a tall mountain range to a flat, swampy plain, perhaps within a period of 15 million years. Fifteen million years is a long time, to be sure, but it is only a fraction of the time that has elapsed since New England's last great geologic upheaval. Had the crust remained stationary, any mountain ranges that resulted from this cataclysm could have been worn away many times over.

That mountains and hills still range across New England, then, is clear evidence that the crust has not remained entirely quiet. Geologists believe that perhaps several times during the millions of centuries that have

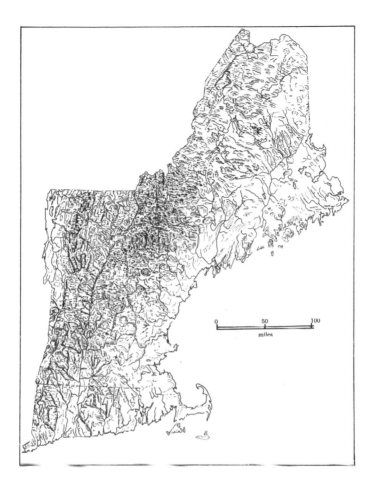

Relief map of New England (after J. R. Illick).

intervened, erosion has reduced the land to an almost flat plain that lay nearly at sea level. Such an erosional plain is known as a *peneplain*.

Between these long periods of erosion, however, there were probably alternate periods when the land gently rose, not with the dramatic folding and faulting that accompanied the earlier uplifts but rather as a broad swelling of the crust across much of the region. As the land rose, the streams that theretofore meandered aimlessly across the flat surface began to quicken and once more started to attack the land, dissecting the peneplain into a region of hills and valleys.

The landscape of southern and central New England was probably formed in this way. Geologists interpret the even horizon as the elevated remnants of a peneplain, that until quite recently in geologic time lay close to sea level. This plain was not entirely flat, however. Here and there across the region were masses of somewhat more durable bedrock that had resisted erosion better than the surrounding land. These now stand as isolated mountains that rise above the lower hills whose even summits mark the elevated peneplain surface. Geologists have given the name *monadnock* to these mountains, after the classic example, Mt. Monadnock.

The uplift that produced today's landscape occurred quite recently in geologic time, probably within the last 8 million years. The entire region bowed upward from about 200 feet near the coast to about 2,000 feet inland. Much of the region is now dissected into hills and valleys, but the Berkshire Hills and the southern end of the Green Mountains are actually a broad plateau which has been deeply cut but nowhere divided by streams. This upland area probably represents the last unbroken remnant of the peneplain.

The peneplain theory has never been proven, nor is it likely ever to be, for the forces of bedrock erosion are far too slow to be perceived in man's brief tenure on earth.

Some investigators have proposed that much of New England was once submerged beneath the sea and that ocean waves, not rivers and streams, leveled the land. This is a definite possibility, but one for which there is now no extant geologic evidence whatsoever. Because of its simplicity, almost all of today's geologists lean toward the peneplain theory rather than that of marine submergence or any of several others.

The courses of several of New England's rivers also indicate that much of the land has only recently risen to its present height. As one might expect, rivers usually carve their valleys through regions of less resistant bedrock. When the erosional cycle is nearly complete, however, and the land has been reduced to a peneplain, the rivers meander sluggishly across areas of hard and soft bedrock alike. If a subsequent uplift is gradual enough and encompasses a wide enough area, as has been the case in New England, many of the rivers will remain essentially in their former courses and deepen their valleys irrespective of the hardness of the bedrock below. As the land around is eroded, the more resistant masses of rock remain as mountains and hills; but these superimposed streams carve valleys across mountain ranges rather than around them.

A number of New England's rivers do just this. In northern New Hampshire, the Androscoggin River has carved a deep valley between the Presidential Range of the White Mountains and its northeastern arm, the Mahoosuc Range. In northern Vermont, both the Winooski and Lamoille Rivers flow westward across the spine of the Green Mountains rather than eastward into the Connecticut River Valley. And the Connecticut River itself, after flowing for most of its course through areas of less resistant bedrock, at Middletown abruptly turns eastward into an area of hard crystalline rock where it has carved a narrow gorge-like valley for the remainder of its course to Long Island Sound.

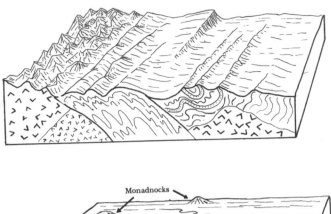

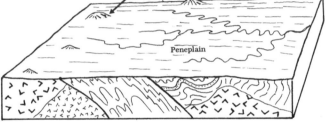

Evolution of the southern New England landscape.
The two block diagrams above show an area of complex
geology similar to that of New England. The upper
drawing shows the area during the early stages of its
development shortly after a period of mountain building.
The lower diagram shows the same area after a long
period of erosion. Streams have gradually reduced the
land to a peneplain. The only elevations remaining
are a few monadnocks.

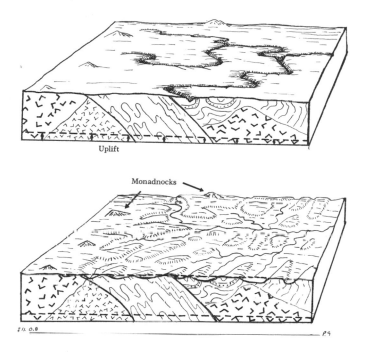

Uplift

Monadnocks

Evolution of the southern New England landscape, continued. The upper drawing shows the same area as that on the opposite page shortly after the crust has arched upward several hundred feet. The streams have responded by carving deep valleys in the peneplain surface. The lower drawing shows the same region a few millions of years later. The streams have now reduced the peneplain surface on the right to a region of hills and valleys whose even summits still mark the peneplain surface. On the left there is still an unbroken portion of the peneplain, which remains as a low plateau. The monadnocks now remain as isolated mountains rising above the hills.

Places to Visit:

Mt. Monadnock, Jaffrey, N.H. (USGS Mt. Monadnock).*
Numerous trails to the summit. Spectacular views. State
Park.

Mt. Wachusett, Princeton, Mass. (USGS Wachusett
Mtn.). Highest mountain in eastern Massachusetts.
Several trails and road to summit. Unsurpassed view of
the peneplain and of other monadnocks. State Park.

Pack Monadnock Mountain, Peterborough, N.H. (USGS
Peterboro). Another monadnock that is accessible by
both road and trail. Part of a line of monadnocks that
extends northward from Mt. Watatic on the Massachusetts border. A hiking trail connects them. State Park.

Mt. Blue, Weld, Maine (USGS Weld). A well-known
monadnock rising above the hilly country of central
Maine. State Park. A booklet of the geology of Mt. Blue
is available from the Maine Dept. of Economic Development, 50¢.

Mt. Ascutney, Windsor, Vt. (USGS Claremont, N.H.). A
3,000-foot monadnock in the Connecticut Valley. Trail
guide available from the Appalachian Mountain Club,
50¢. State Park.

Mt. Sunapee, Sunapee, N.H. (USGS Sunapee).
Mt. Cardigan, Orange, N.H. (USGS Cardigan).
Mt. Kearsarge, Wilmot Flat, N.H. (USGS Mt. Kearsarge). Three monadnocks in southwestern New Hampshire. All are state parks.

*Topographic map reference. See appendix for information
on how to use topographic maps and where to order them.

Books to Read:

Regional Geomorphology of the United States by William D. Thornbury (Wiley, 1965). An excellent interpretation of the landscape of the U.S. In the New England section, there is a good discussion of its erosional history.

Physiography of the United States by Charles B. Hunt (Freeman, 1967). Another excellent summary of the physical features of the U.S. Somewhat less technical than Thornbury's book. Some information on plant geography included. (Out of Print)

Geographical Essays by W. M. Davis (Dover, 1957). A reprint of a collection of essays written by the "father of the peneplain concept."

Geology of the Mount Monadnock Quadrangle by Katherine Fowler-Billings (available from New Hampshire Dept. of Economic Development, $1.00). Geological explanation of the Monadnock region. Semi-technical.

*Mailing addresses for obtaining this and other publications not generally for sale in bookstores are listed in the appendix.

The Green Mountains and
Berkshire Hills

From the summit of Mt. Monadnock on a clear day, it is possible to see a large section of Vermont's Green Mountains. In contrast to the bumpy skyline of the White Mountains to the north, the westward view toward Vermont presents a remarkably even horizon — the remnants of the peneplain — broken only here and there by an occasional monadnock. The even skyline of the Green Mountains is more reminiscent of Virginia's Blue Ridge than any of New England's other mountains. And well it should be, for both the Blue Ridge and the Green Mountains are truncated remnants of long north-south-running folds in the bedrock crust.

Today's Green Mountains are merely the deeply eroded roots of a very old mountain range, the oldest in New England for which any clear geologic record remains. Geologists believe that the ancestral Green Mountains first appeared about 440 million years ago. Four hundred and forty million is a vast length of time, to be sure, but it is less than one-tenth of the total age of the earth; so much time had already passed that several earlier mountain ranges, one after another, might have pushed skyward, then disappeared without a trace, right on the site of today's mountains.

When geologists speak of the Green Mountains or any other mountain range as being old, they are not implying that the present landscape, the mountains and valleys that we view today, is particularly old. What they are referring to is the date of the origin of the mountains. The previous section has shown that New England's present skyline is relatively youthful, probably at the most only a few million years old. Even this comparatively

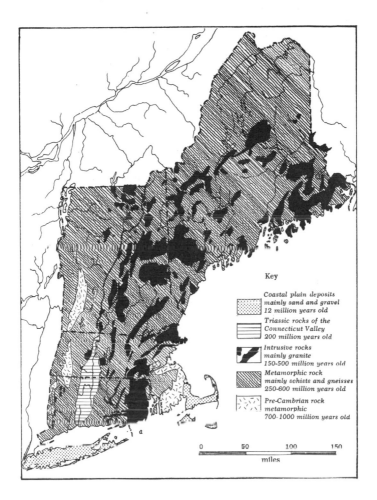

Key

Coastal plain deposits
mainly sand and gravel
12 million years old

Triassic rocks of the
Connecticut Valley
200 million years old

Intrusive rocks
mainly granite
150-500 million years old

Metamorphic rock
mainly schists and gneisses
250-600 million years old

Pre-Cambrian rock
metamorphic
700-1000 million years old

| 0 | 50 | 100 | 150 |

miles

Geologic map of New England (after E-an Zen, et al.).

short period of time has been long enough to allow the extremely slow forces of erosion and uplift to bring vast changes to the face of the land. In the 440 million years that have elapsed since the ancestral Green Mountains first appeared, erosion has stripped away a total of perhaps 6 miles of bedrock from the present mountain surface.

South of Rutland, the Green Mountains form a large, unbroken upland area extending southward to the Massachusetts border. This plateau is about 20 miles wide in the vicinity of Stratton Mountain, one of the monadnocks that rise above it. To both the north and the south it narrows down. It is in this area that erosion has exposed the mountain core, a complex of billion-year-old rocks that rank among New England's oldest.

North of Rutland, the Green Mountains become three distinct parallel mountain ranges. Their skylines become more rugged and the individual mountain peaks higher and more numerous. Here are the highest of the Green Mountains: Mt. Killington, Mt. Ellen, The Camel's Hump, and Mt. Mansfield — all above 4,000 feet.

The Berkshire Hills are closely related to the Green Mountains. Both are part of a large upfold that extends from central Pennsylvania through southern New York State and western New England well into Canada. The underlying rocks of the Berkshires, and their structure, though not exactly the same as the Green Mountains, are nevertheless quite similar.

In addition, the appearance of the present-day Berkshire Hills differs from that of the Green Mountains only in degree. As was mentioned in the first section, both are remnants of the uplifted New England peneplain, the upland surface of the Berkshires being only a few hundred feet lower than the Green Mountains, and the isolated monadnocks appearing as hardly more than hills rising above the elevated surface. The plateau-like character of the Berkshire Hills may be clearly seen by driving across them. The Massachusetts Turnpike climbs gradually westward from the Connecticut Valley, crossing several deeply cut river valleys on the way. After about 25 miles, in the town of Becket, there is a sign on the roadside stating that the highway has reached its highest point. From here the land stretches away to an almost flat horizon. It is only the rather northern flavor of the woods, the spruce and balsam, that gives the traveler any clue that he has reached a fairly high elevation.

The drive up Route 2 in northern Massachusetts, the Mohawk Trail, illustrates even better the steep-sided, plateau-like appearance of the Berkshires. From the Connecticut River the highway stays in the valleys, first along the Deerfield River, then up an impressive gorge formed by a tributary stream, the Cold River. The highway finally twists and turns itself free of the deep valley and climbs steeply to the top of the plateau. For 5 miles the highway crosses a landscape hardly more hilly than that of eastern Massachusetts, until it reaches the western edge of the Berkshires, where it abruptly drops 1,000 feet to North Adams and the Hoosac River Valley below. The views from this road at both the eastern and the western edges of the Berkshires are impressive, particularly the western view, for directly opposite, rising abruptly behind North Adams, is Mt. Greylock, the highest point in Massachusetts.

The Green Mountain-Berkshire upland area is deeply cut by valleys but is nowhere broken through for nearly 170 miles. It is not surprising that it presented a formidable barrier to westward travel for many years. There are still relatively few roads across the area and all are steep. The builders of the railroad westward from Boston did not attempt to lay tracks over the 2,000 foot high upland, but instead blasted a six-mile-long tunnel through it near the Mohawk Trail. When it was completed in 1874, the Hoosac Tunnel was acclaimed to be one of the engineering wonders of the day.

Places to Visit:

Mt. Mansfield, Stowe, Vt. (USGS Mt. Mansfield). Highest mountain in the state. Trails, ski lifts, toll road to summit. On a clear day it is possible to see Mt. Washington to the east and Lake Champlain and the Adirondacks to the west.

Long Trail. A wilderness trail along the crest of the Green Mountains from one end of the state to the other. Lean-tos spaced for a convenient day's hike. *Long Trail Guide*, 19th ed., 1968 (available from Appalachian Mountain Club, $1.95).

Route 100. Scenic winding road along the eastern side of the Green Mountains almost from one end of Vermont to the other.

White Rocks near Wallingford, Vt. (USGS Wallingford). Western scarp of the Green Mountains, bold cliff of almost snow-white quartzite.

Books to Read:

Studies of Appalachian Geology, Northern and Maritime ed. by E-an Zen, W. S. White, J. B. Hadley, & J. B. Thompson, Jr. (Wiley, 1968). A comprehensive review of the present state of knowledge of the exceedingly complex geology of the Appalachian Mountains. Technical, but of great value to any person seriously interested in the geology of this region. The references include practically every scientific article published on the geology of the northern Appalachians. (Out of Print)

The Friendly Mountains ed. by Roderick Peattie (Vanguard Press, 1942). A somewhat dated though interesting account of the Green Mountains, White Mountains, Adirondacks, and Taconics — both their natural and their human histories. (Out of Print)

The Berkshires ed. by Roderick Peattie (Vanguard Press, 1948). A similar book on the western Massachusetts mountains. Some of the geology is out of date. (Out of Print)

The Physical Features of Vermont by Elbridge Churchhill Jacobs, 1950 (available from Vermont State Library, $1.00). Describes the various physiographic regions of Vermont. Also contains a simple explanation of the state's geology.

Geological Map of Vermont, ed. by Charles C. Doll, 1961 (available from Vermont State Library, $4.00). A large up-to-date geological map of the state. Useful to anyone with a serious interest in bedrock geology of Vermont.

Paleontology of the Champlain Basin in Vermont by Charles W. Welby, 1962 (available from Vermont State Library, $2.00). Information for fossil hunting in the Champlain region.

In addition, the Vermont Geological Survey has made geologic maps of a number of USGS quadrangles together with an explanatory bulletin on each. These are somewhat technical for the layman but may be of local interest. A list of publications is available from the Vermont State Library, Montpelier, Vermont.

The Taconic Mountains

Route 7 parallels the western edge of the Green Mountains. Driving north, the traveler is constantly aware of the unbroken, flattish mountain mass to his right. In southern Vermont and much of Massachusetts there is also a range of mountains — more "mountain-like" in appearance — on the traveler's left. These are the Taconic Mountains, a narrow range that straddles the New York-New England border from northern Connecticut to central Vermont.

In contrast to the unbroken, flat-topped Green Mountains, the Taconics are deeply cut into peaks and valleys. Both the Hoosac River in northwestern Massachusetts and Batten Kill in southwestern Vermont have cut deep valleys through the range. Vermont's Mt. Equinox and Mt. Greylock in Massachusetts are the highest of several peaks along the Taconic Range. Rising as they do from the deep valley, they assume a more impressive appearance than some of the higher Green Mountain peaks that rise above the 2,000 foot high plateau.

The Taconic Mountains seem intimately related to the Green Mountains, but for years the question of how they were formed was one of the great geologic mysteries of New England. Although the matter has not yet been definitely settled, the present consensus among geologists is that the ancient Taconic Mountains literally slid off the top of the Green Mountains. Crustal folding became so intense along the Green Mountains that the whole top of the fold — of which the present-day Taconics are probably only a small remaining part — actually broke off the mountain mass and slid westward a distance of 10 or 15 miles to their present position.

The Lone Rock Point thrust fault, Burlington, Vermont. See description in text.

In addition to the Taconics, there are a number of other places in western New England where large blocks of bedrock broke loose and moved sideways. This type of geologic process — the breaking and lateral movement of the bedrock — is called a *thrust fault*. Most of these thrust faults lie buried beneath the glacial debris; where they are exposed, it often takes a trained eye to detect and interpret them. At Lone Rock Point just north of Burlington, Vermont, however, there is one of the most clearly seen and easily understood examples of a thrust fault in the whole country. Here on the shore of Lake Champlain a massive block of dolomite, a limestone-like sedimentary rock, can be seen jutting out over a bed of much younger shale. Since older rocks usually lie under younger rocks, geologists infer that some distance to the east the layered rocks cracked, and the upper block, of which the dolomite is a part, gradually rode up and over the younger shale.

A long and almost continuous valley separates the Taconic Mountains from the Green Mountains and the Berkshire Hills to the east. North of Rutland, beyond the end of the Taconics, the valley widens out into the broad lowland that is occupied in part by Lake Champlain. To the south, except for an intervening ridge near the Vermont-Massachusetts state line, the valley runs without a break all the way to northern Connecticut.

About 1,500 feet lower than the mountains on either side for most of its length, this valley clearly illustrates the relationship of the bedrock to the landscape. In contrast to the harder rocks of the mountains on either side, the rock under the valley and the lowland to the north is mostly limestone, marble, and other closely related rock. All of these rocks are comparatively soft, and all are more or less soluble in ground water. In areas having high rainfall like New England, these rocks are among the least resistant. As a consequence, areas underlain by limestone usually erode more rapidly than those where the bedrock is of another type. The result may be a valley or lowland similar to what has formed in western New England.

Beneath that portion of the valley running from Dorset, Vermont, northward to Brandon lie virtually all of New England's commercial marble deposits.

Marble is limestone that heat and pressure deep within the earth have transformed from its usually dull, lusterless state into a sparkling, crystalline substance. The process by which the character of a rock is changed radically by such forces is called *metamorphism*. It is only in that small part of the valley described above that geologic conditions combined to produce commercially valuable marble. Marble occurs from one end of the limestone area to the other; it is possible to find lumps of marble in the stone walls along the roadside and to see whitish, weathered outcrops of the rock here and there throughout the limestone valley and Champlain Lowland, but most of this marble is of indifferent quality, almost always unsuitable for building or statuary.

Vermont is the second largest marble producer in the nation: virtually all of its marble comes from this region. From Route 7 it is possible to see a number of quarries and prospect pits throughout this area. Large quarries still operate in Danby, West Rutland, and Proctor.

Pure marble is snow-white; its various colors and patterns are caused by small amounts of impurities. Even within Vermont there are great differences in the color of the marble from one locality to another. For example, the quarries at Danby produce a pure, snow-white marble; at Proctor the marble has grayish bands; a beautiful black marble was formerly quarried on the Isle La Motte in Lake Champlain. Other Vermont quarries have produced both greenish and reddish marble.

At Proctor, the Vermont Marble Company maintains

a large marble exhibit showing the geology, quarrying, and carving of this ornamental stone.

Westland Marble Quarry, West Rutland, Vermont.

Places to Visit:

Mt. Equinox, Manchester, Vt. (USGS Equinox). Highest mountain in the Taconic Range. Toll road to the summit. Excellent views of the Taconics, the Valley of Vermont, and the Green Mountains.

Thrust fault, Lone Rock Point, Burlington, Vt. (USGS Plattsburgh, N.Y.). Located on shores of Lake Champlain just north of Burlington Bay on land owned by Episcopal Diocese. Said to be one of the finest examples of a thrust fault to be seen in the U.S.

Slate mining district, West Pawlet to West Castleton, Vt. (USGS Pawlet & Castleton). Huge piles of slate on either side of Route 22A.

Marble quarries in the Valley of Vermont from Dorset northward to Shelburne. Visitors are not permitted at working quarries but there are dozens of abandoned marble quarries in the district that can be explored.

Marble exhibit at Proctor, Vt. Vermont Marble Company maintains an exhibit of the geology, quarrying, and the uses of marble. Samples of marble from many different localities both in Vermont and elsewhere.

Aerial view of the White Mountains, south from Crawford Notch.

The White Mountains

"The only fault I find with New Hampshire," wrote Robert Frost, "is that her mountains aren't quite high enough." It is true that New Hampshire's White Mountains suffer by comparison with our western mountains, that 6,000-foot Mt. Washington is less than half the elevation of Colorado's Pikes Peak; yet the White Mountains do provide the most rugged scenery anywhere in the eastern two-thirds of the nation and are sufficiently impressive to attract many thousands of visitors each year.

Like the Green Mountains to the west, the White Mountains are the deeply eroded roots of what were probably much higher mountains in times past; but here practically all similarities between the two mountain groups end. When viewed from a distance, the Green Mountains across much of their range present a smooth, nearly horizontal profile. By contrast, the skyline of the White Mountains is bumpy and irregular. The Green Mountains form a narrow, clearly delineated range running northward from Massachusetts, through Vermont, into Canada; the White Mountains, on the other hand, form a disorderly group that centers in north-central New Hampshire, with outlying mountains straggling off for many miles in several directions. Furthermore, the topography of the Green Mountains — the long ridges and plateau-like uplands — closely reflects the structure of the folded rock layers below, whereas the topography of the White Mountains is only partially related to the structure of the underlying bedrock.

The geology of the White Mountains is extremely complex. The bedrock shows evidence of many of the same forces that molded the Green Mountains: uplift, folding, and faulting; likewise intense heat and pressure deep within the earth have metamorphosed the rocks and destroyed most of the fossil record. In addition, however, the White Mountain region has been the scene of intense *igneous* activity, by which great masses of molten rock have welled up into the layered rocks above where they solidified to form granite and other related rock.

So widespread was this igneous activity that nearly one-third of all New Hampshire's rock is granite or a related type of igneous rock. Thus, New Hampshire's nickname, "The Granite State," is an apt one. Although these giant bodies of granite trail off from New Hampshire into

Maine, Massachusetts, and northeastern Vermont, nowhere in these other states do they cover such an extensive area as they do in New Hampshire.

Granite from Conway, New Hampshire.
The black grains are crystals of black
mica; the white, feldspar; and the gray,
smoky quartz.

The size of the mineral grains in an igneous rock gives some clue as to its origin. Molten rock that penetrated nearly to the surface or spewed forth as lava cooled rapidly and hence is fine-grained. On the other hand, rock that slowly cooled and crystallized deep within the earth's interior, *plutonic rock* in the geologist's parlance, is usually made up of coarse, easily distinguishable mineral grains. Granite, the most familiar of the coarse-grained plutonic rock, is only one of the many different types found in New England.

That these rocks, probably formed miles underground, are now exposed on the surface gives us some idea of how much erosion must have taken place over the eons of geologic time. But the relationship between these bodies of plutonic rock and today's mountain topography is complex. Granite and related rocks are usually more resistant to erosion that most other types of rock. Indeed, much of the mountainous part of New Hampshire is underlain by granite; likewise, the bedrock of the Katahdin Range in central Maine is also largely granite. In other places not too distant from the White Mountains, however, granite bodies similar to those that form the mountains have, surprisingly enough, eroded faster than the surrounding rock and now are areas of lakes and swampland.

Furthermore, there are a number of peaks in the White Mountains where the rocks are not granitic at all. The highest of the White Mountains, the Presidential Range which includes Mt. Washington, are built not of granite or some other plutonic rock but of a combination of several types of metamorphic rock. Mt. Moosilauke and Mt. Monadnock to the south are also resistant masses of metamorphic rock. In other areas nearby, however, the same rock types have been eroded away. It must be said, then, that the relationship of the type of bedrock in the region to its present-day topography is not easily explained.

*Giant conglomerate along Route 128,
Milton, Massachusetts. Rounded boulders
washed into place by an ancient mountain
stream. A geologist's pick for scale is
shown in the lower right hand corner.*

During the time of the formation of the ancient White Mountains, high mountains probably existed in southern New England as well. A giant *conglomerate* of this age, containing large round boulders similar to those found in mountain streams, outcrops near Blue Hill south of Boston. Other evidence for high mountains in the Boston area includes a layer of *tillite,* glacial debris now solid rock, believed to have been formed by glaciers flowing off these mountains. The tillite lies interbedded with other rocks of this age and could not possibly be confused with the widespread glacial deposits of much more recent times.

Today's White Mountain landscape is far more subdued than it must have been in those early days. Here, as elsewhere in New England, the landscape is the result of gentle uplift and consequent erosion. Geologists believe that what is now the White Mountain region has remained quiet for the last quarter billion years; practically all of the great geologic activity — the folding and faulting that bent and tore the rocks and the great plutons of molten rock that welled up into the crust — took place before that time. What we now see as the White Mountains, like the neighboring Green Mountains to the west, are merely the roots of much greater mountains that have slowly worn away over the tremendous passage of time.

Places to Visit:

Mt. Washington (USGS Mt. Washington). Highest mountain in New England. Fresh exposures of the metamorphic rock that underlies the mountain may be seen along the carriage road.

South Moat Mountain (USGS North Conway). Large exposure of the volcanic rock that perhaps overspread all of New Hampshire at one time. Best exposures lie along the South Moat Trail and Spur Trail one-half mile west of the mountain.

Mt. Chocorua (USGS Mt. Chocorua). Granite peak on the southern flank of the White Mountains.

Kankamagus Highway (USGS Crawford Notch and Franconia). Scenic route from Conway to Woodstock, N.H. For almost its entire distance, the highway crosses the largest of the plutonic bodies that form the core of the southern White Mountains. Almost all of the bedrock along the route is granite.

The Flume (USGS Franconia). Gorge formed in an eroded basalt dike. (See page 53.)

Mt. Katahdin (USGS Mt. Katahdin). Seventeen miles north of Millinocket, Maine. Mt. Katahdin and the other southern peaks in the range are entirely composed of gray or pink granite. The bedrock of the northern part of the range is rhyolite, a light-colored igneous rock of the same composition as granite.

Granite quarries near Barre, Vt. (USGS Barre). Several granite quarries are still in operation. Observation platform and guided tours. There are other working granite quarries in each of the New England states except Rhode Island.

Note. Other places of interest in the White Mountain region are listed in later sections.

Books to Read:

The Geology of New Hampshire: Part II, Bedrock Geology by Marland P. Billings (available from New Hampshire Dept. of Resources and Economic Development).

A detailed summary of the bedrock geology of the state. Some sections require a knowledge of geology; others are understandable to the layman. A large map of New Hampshire's bedrock geology comes with the text or may be purchased separately. (Out of Print)

Studies of Appalachian Geology, Northern and Maritime. See description p. 18.

The Mountains of New Hampshire (available from New Hampshire Dept. of Resources and Economic Development, 50¢). A directory locating the mountains and prominent elevations in the state. (Out of Print)

In addition there are detailed geologic maps and reports of the geology of most of the USGS quadrangles of New Hampshire. A list is available from the above address. These are somewhat technical but may be of local interest to the layman.

A.M.C. White Mountain Guide, 1976 (available from Appalachian Mountain Club, $8 plus tax). Hikers' guide to all the mountains of New Hampshire. Maps and descriptions of trails.

A.M.C. Guide to Mt. Washington and the Presidential Range by Howard Goff. 1977 (available from Appalachian Mountain Club, $3.95 plus tax). Includes trail guide and information on Mountain Ecosystems, weather, management, etc.

A.M.C. Trail Guide to Mt. Desert and Acadia National Park, 1975 (available from Appalachian Mountain Club, $2.00 plus tax).

A.M.C. Maine Mountain Guide, 2nd ed., 1976 (available from Appalachian Mountain Club, $6.50 plus tax). Hikers' guide to the mountains of Maine with special attention given the Katahdin and Mt. Desert Regions. Separate maps available for both Katahdin and Mt. Desert Island ($1.00 each).

Fifty Hikes in the White Mountains by Daniel Doan (New Hampshire Publishing Co., Somersworth, N.H., 1975). Guide to 50 day and backpacking hikes in the White Mountains. Detailed maps, superb photographs.

Geologic Map of Maine, 1967 (available from the Maine Department of Economic Development, $4.00). A large-scale, full-color map of Maine's bedrock geology shows the continuation of the White Mountain bedrock formations across Maine.

Maine Granite Quarries and Prospects by Muriel B. Austin and Arthur M. Hussey II, 1958 (available from Maine Department of Economic Development, $1.00 plus tax).

The Connecticut Valley Lowland

The Connecticut Valley Lowland splits southern New England neatly in two. Like a giant wedge, the corridor stretches from the Connecticut coast 100 miles northward, where it narrows to a point near the Massachusetts-New Hampshire state line. As its name implies, the lowland is lower by several hundred feet than the hill country on either side. At Hartford, the valley floor is still only a few feet above sea level; on either side the land gently rises, often in a series of low, step-like terraces, to the sharper slopes of the bordering upland.

The lowland is not, however, a uniformly gentle landscape. Throughout the region a series of craggy ridges rises abruptly from its basin-like floor. Nowhere are these hills more than a few hundred feet higher than the surrounding land, yet they offer a pleasing contrast to the otherwise bland scenery. One slope of each of these hills, usually to the north or west, is steep — often cliff-like — with piles of *talus*, broken rock that has fallen from it, lying below. In contrast, the opposite slope is gentle, giving the hill an asymmetric, sawtooth profile.

One of the most striking features of the Connecticut Lowland, one that clearly sets it apart from the rest of New England, is the reddish color of its soil. The color is not surprising, for most of the underlying bedrock is also red. In contrast to the hard grayish schists and gneisses that underlie the land around it, the red rocks of the lowland are softer sandstones and shales that crumble easily into soil. The comparative softness of its rock is undoubtedly a reason why the area is now lower than its surroundings.

The geologic history of the Connecticut Lowland with its reddish rocks and oddly shaped hills is one of the

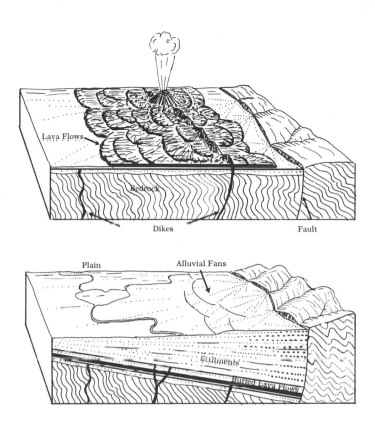

Lava Flows

Bedrock

Dikes   Fault

Plain   Alluvial Fans

Sediments

Buried Lava Flows

Geologic evolution of the Connecticut Valley. The two block diagrams above show a portion of the valley during the early stages of its development about 200 million years ago. A major fault occurred along the eastern side of the valley. West of the fault line, a block of the crust is slowly moving downward and the depression is becoming filled with layer after layer of sediments interspersed with three lava flows.

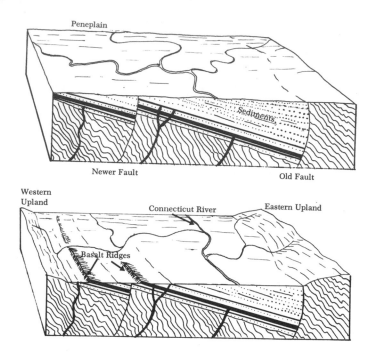

Peneplain

Newer Fault

Old Fault

Western Upland

Connecticut River

Eastern Upland

Basalt Ridges

Sediments

Geologic evolution of the Connecticut Valley, continued. The top diagram shows the area in comparatively recent times, about 2 million years ago. Erosion has reduced the land to a peneplain (see page 20). Streams meander aimlessly across the nearly-flat surface of the land. The lower diagram shows the same portion of the valley as it appears today. The crust has risen and streams have once more begun eroding the land, wearing away first the soft sandstones and shales and leaving the more resistant volcanic layers as sharp hills.

most interesting in New England. It began about 200 million years ago, when a fault occurred along what is now the eastern side of the lowland. As the earth's crust cracked, the land east of the fault slowly rose into a range of mountains.

As the range slowly appeared east of the fault line, streams began to carve valleys in its flanks. The broken and decayed bedrock washed off the mountains and accumulated in broad semicircular deposits called *alluvial fans*. The coarse material came to rest near the apex of the fan while the finer material traveled outward toward its margins. Because the Connecticut Lowland sediments are thicker and coarser along their eastern margin, there is no doubt that they came from that direction.

At three different times, outpourings of lava spread across the basin and interrupted the accumulation of sediments. A layer of volcanic bombs and ash in the Holyoke region indicates that here the lava flows were accompanied by violent volcanic activity. Elsewhere, however, the lava probably flowed quietly from fissures in the underlying rock. Almost before the lava sheets cooled, the sedimentary deposition resumed.

As the sedimentary layers continued to pile up west of the fault line, the crust beneath them began to subside. A long block comprising what is now the entire Connecticut Lowland slowly dropped like a giant trap door, hinged somewhere to the west and opening downward along the fault line. As a result, the sediments and hardened lava flows in this part of the basin became gently tipped. A similar but much smaller subsidence took place in the area that is now the Pomperaug Valley, near Woodbury, Connecticut, about 10 miles west of the lowland, and a third yet smaller subsidence occurred in what is now the Cherry Brook Valley near Canton, Connecticut.

The sediments in the valley gradually hardened into rock. The sand became sandstone; the gravel, conglomerate; and the clay, shale. Meanwhile, the lava flows had hardened into a dark gray rock called *basalt*. Finally, some minor faults broke up the layers of sediments into a series of small blocks that also tipped downward to the east.

A long period of erosion followed. Running water and weather gradually destroyed all vestiges of the mountains east of the fault and removed all of the sedimentary rock to the west, except that tipped downward in the subsided blocks that now form the Connecticut Lowland, the Pomperaug Valley, and the Cherry Brook Valley. The same sequence of sediments and all three lava flows appears in the Pomperaug Valley, evidence that this basin once stretched far beyond its present limits.

Knowing something of the lowland's geologic history makes it easier to understand the present-day landscape. Because the tilted basalt layers are more resistant to weather and erosion than the soft sandstones, shales, and conglomerates, they now rise above the lowland floor as the sharp ridges described earlier. Basalt usually breaks perpendicularly; this explains the formation of cliffs and steep slopes on one side of these hills. The gentle slope on the opposite side reflects the tilt of the basalt strata. As one might expect, the thickest basalt layer, the middle one, has produced the highest hills. Totoket Mountain, near New Haven; the Hanging Hills of Meriden; Talcott Mountain west of Hartford; and several other ridges in the lowland are all remnants of the middle flow.

The lowest, and now westernmost, basalt sheet thins out and disappears in northern Connecticut while the other two run northward into Massachusetts where they become the Mt. Tom-Holyoke Range. Here the upper sheet ends. The middle sheet reaches the northern end of the lowland where it gives substance to the Pocumtuck Hills from Deerfield to Gill.

West Rock, another basalt ridge, rises abruptly in the northern end of New Haven and runs northward about 20 miles to Southington. Many New Englanders will remember this rugged little basalt ridge, for the Wilbur Cross Highway tunnels through it just north of New Haven. Unlike the tilted basalt hills that are steep on one side and gentle on the other, West Rock is equally steep on both sides. This different structure suggests a different mode of formation. Geologists believe that West Rock is one of several large *dikes* in the lowland region. A dike is formed — usually deep in the earth — when lava squeezes up into a more or less vertical crack in the crust above. Some of these dikes remain underground; others may appear on the earth's surface after erosion has stripped away the overlying rock.

Basalt dikes are quite common in many parts of New England. However, most are only a few feet wide and probably solidified far underground. The several-hundred-foot thickness of the West Rock dike, on the other hand, leads geologists to infer that the crack in which it was formed was a major fissure, and the molten rock may well have reached the surface and poured out across the land. Thus West Rock may have been a feeder to one of the lava flows that now form the tilted hills. As in these other hills, the hardness of the basalt has resisted erosion better than the surrounding sandstones and now stands 400 feet above the surrounding land. Another long dike runs from Unionville to Granby in northern Connecticut, and many smaller ones cut the lowland sediments as well as the older rocks on either side of the Connecticut Lowland.

Although these basalt hills dominate the region's landscape, it is the less spectacular sedimentary rocks, the sandstones and shales, that may command the greater geologic interest. Etched in their layers is a fascinating history of those ancient times. Ripple marks hardened in the rock show where a small stream meandered across the land; mudcracks, now polygonal designs in the shale, mark the dried up bottoms of small ponds; even the spatter of raindrops from a passing shower remain preserved in the rock — all reminders that the same geologic processes of today were taking place 200 million years ago.

But even more fascinating is the abundant record of animal life. Imprinted in the rocks from one end of the lowland to the other are thousands of animal tracks, tracks far different from those of any animal of today. For most of these animals, their tracks are the only record we have; of the 150 species that have been identified from their tracks, fossilized bones of only 14 have been unearthed in the Connecticut Valley so far. The fine-grained shales from the northern end of the lowland have also yielded a variety of invertebrate tracks, mostly insects and wormlike animals, but as in the case of the vertebrate trackmakers, actual remains are rare.

Yet, much information about these animals can be gleaned from the tracks alone; by comparing them to the fossilized remains of similar animals found elsewhere, paleontologists are able to make some informed guesses as to what these ancient animals looked like. For example, some trackmakers were animals that walked on all fours; others moved on their hind legs only.

Early geologists interpreted the two-legged trackmakers as being large birds, but later evidence has shown that birds did not come upon the scene until millions of years later. Now geologists are quite certain that all of the larger trackmakers were reptiles, some crawling on all fours, others walking upright on their hind legs alone.

Dinosaur footprints in shale, Granby, Massachusetts. Early geologists thought that the three-toed dinosaurs were large birds. Tracks have been darkened with oil to make them more easily visible in the rock. The ball-point pens give scale.

Other inferences may be gathered from the tracks. The size of the tracks is related to the size of the track-maker; the distance between each track, to the length of his legs; and the width of the trackways gives a rough idea of his body width. From the tracks it appears that most of these early dinosaurs were smaller than a man — in contrast to the giant dinosaurs that reached their greatest size about 100 million years later — though a few of these early specimens may have reached a length of 20 feet.

Slabs of track-bearing rock adorn the walls of practically every geological museum in the east. The best local collections are on display at Amherst College, Mount Holyoke College, and Yale. Tracks may also be seen *in situ* in three places in the lowland area: near Smith's Ferry and South Hadley in Massachusetts and in Rocky Hill, Connecticut.

The Smith's Ferry locality is owned by the Massachusetts Trustees of Reservations and is just off Route 5 about a mile south of the entrance to Mt. Tom Reservation. A seven-acre area of exposed ledge shows tracks of about a dozen different species of dinosaurs. As is common with most unguarded areas of natural interest, these tracks have suffered somewhat from vandalism.

Another footprint locality, the Nash Quarry, is about a half mile east of Route 116 near the South Hadley-Granby town line. At the present time, the quarry is the only commercial source of footprints. It has produced many of the track slabs seen in the museums, and tracks are for sale here.

The most recently discovered footprint locality, Dinosaur State Park in Rocky Hill, Connecticut, was found by accident. In 1966, workmen uncovered the tracks on state property during the excavation for a highway department laboratory. Quick action by geologists, conservationists, and state legislators had this area declared a state park and the laboratory was built elsewhere.

A rich footprint area lies along the Connecticut River in Gill, Massachusetts, from the French King Bridge three and one-half miles westward to the basalt scarp of the Pocumtuck Hills. Various spots along this stretch of the river have yielded footprints of over 100 different reptiles and amphibian species, abundant plant fossils, and virtually all the known invertebrate tracks, mostly those of insects and worms. Route 2 runs along the north side of the river through the same fossil-bearing strata. Several exposed ledges along the highway have also yielded tracks.

This area, both along the river banks during low water and along the roadside, is probably the richest collecting ground for the amateur fossil hunter. The tracks are not common but do occur frequently enough to reward a diligent search. The shale weathers rather quickly and splits into thin slabs. A stout hammer, some cold chisels, and a small pick for prying loose the weathered rock are the necessary tools. Rubber-soled shoes or sneakers for climbing the inclined beds are also essential.

The dinosaurs left a wide variety of tracks of different sizes and shapes; many of the tracks are indistinct and shallow. Therefore, it is easy to overlook them, especially the smaller ones. An excellent guide and pictured key to the dinosaur tracks and the other Connecticut Valley fossils is listed at the end of this section.

Although dinosaurs roamed the valley for perhaps millions of years, their tracks are only clearly preserved in relatively few of the many layers of sediments that gradually accumulated on the valley floor. Practically all of the really clear footprints come from layers of fine-grained rock, mostly shale.

How tracks got into the middle of hard rock requires a note of explanation. Two hundred million years ago, the sedimentary layers were still soft. The shale of today was mud on the bottom of shallow, intermittent ponds. As these ponds were drying out, dinosaurs and other animals walked across them leaving their footprints in the mud. The mud dried out completely and was baked by the sun. The next rainstorm refilled the ponds and washed a new layer of mud across the hardened tracks, burying them before they could soften and wash away. The continued accumulation of sediments gradually squeezed the track-bearing sediments together, hardening them into rock.

The curious reddish color of the Connecticut Valley shales and sandstones is primarily the result of the climate rather than any property of the sediments themselves. Extensive areas of reddish soils cover areas of the present-day tropics, regions which have a generally high temperature and at least periodic high humidity but receive only seasonal rainfall. From this and other evidence, geologists have inferred that the landscape during those ancient times was probably similar to the present-day tropical savanna, an open, occasionally swampy plain. The rocks have yielded enough woody plant fossils to indicate that at least some of the area was wooded, probably that adjacent to the main watercourses. The very abundance of tracks is also evidence that there had to be vegetation to feed at least some of the trackmakers; they could not all have been flesh eaters.

The Connecticut Valley today is a far different scene from the tropical savannas and swamplands of 200 million years ago. Much of the lowland is rich farmland, the open fields providing a pleasing contrast to the wooded uplands on either side. The countryside lacks the rugged grandeur of the mountain areas to the north, but is interesting to the casual tourist as well as the geologist. It is possible to cover the whole length of the lowland nonstop in two hours, and to follow the Connecticut River northward to the Canadian border in less than a day. It is possible, but in doing so, the traveler will miss most of the picturesque charm this region has to offer. Far more worthwhile is a leisurely drive up the secondary roads, through unspoiled valley towns with their well-kept houses, village greens, and white churches. Traveling this way, it is easy to detour to places of natural or historical interest along the way. The Connecticut Valley is regarded by many as New England's most scenic region.

Places to Visit:

The following parks and reservations are located on the basalt hills in the Connecticut Lowland. All show interesting rock formations and many excellent views from high points:

Mt. Tom State Reservation, Easthampton, Mass. (USGS Easthampton). Entrance off Route 5 at Smith's Ferry.

Joseph A. Skinner State Park, Hadley, Mass (USGS Mt. Holyoke). Off Route 47, north of South Hadley.

Penwood State Park, Bloomfield, Conn. (USGS Avon). Off Route 185, east of Weatogue.

West Peak State Park, Meriden, Conn. (USGS Meriden). Entrance through Hubbard Park off Route 6A in the northwest corner of Meriden.

Trimountain State Park, Durham, Conn. (USGS Wallingford and Mt. Carmel). Off Route 10, north of Mt. Carmel.

Mt. Sugarloaf State Reservation, Sunderland, Mass. (USGS Mt. Toby). A steep-sided hill, not of basalt but of sandstone, rising out of the lowland floor. Road to summit.

West Rock Park, New Haven, Conn. (USGS New Haven). See description in text.

Dinosaur Track Localities:

Dinosaur State Park, Rocky Hill, Conn. (USGS Hartford South). See description in text.

Dinosaur Footprints, Smith's Ferry, Mass. (USGS Easthampton). See description in text.

Nash Quarry, Granby, Mass. See description in text.

Track Area, Route 2, Gill, Mass. (USGS Greenfield). See description in text.

Museums with Track Collections:

Peabody Museum, Yale University, New Haven, Conn.

Geological Museum, Amherst College, Amherst, Mass.

Bed of Connecticut River below Holyoke Dam, Holyoke, Mass. During low water several acres of riverbed are exposed. The area is an outdoor geological museum showing dozens of different geologic features. Guide to the area with map and photographs in *Economic Geology* of *Massachusetts* ed. by O. C. Farquar (see p. 65).

Books to Read:

The Flow of Time in the Connecticut Valley, 2nd ed., by G. W. Bain & H. A. Meyerhoff (Connecticut Valley Historical Museum, Springfield, Mass. 1963). Discusses the bedrock and surficial geology of the Connecticut Valley in layman's terms. (Out of Print)

Triassic Life in the Connecticut Valley, Bulletin 81, by Richard Swann Lull (Connecticut Geological and Natural History Survey, 1953). Pictured key to footprints and discussion of the fossilized dinosaur remains. Maps show footprint localities. (Out of Print)

Fossils of the Connecticut Valley, Bulletin 97, by Edwin H. Colbert (Connecticut Geological and Natural History Survey). Non-technical guide to the fossils and fossil localities in the valley. Good discussion of the geology.

New England's Mineral Resources

Most people associate rocky land with mineral wealth. Considering how rocky New England is, one might expect to find a flourishing mining industry here. Nothing could be further from the fact. New England is more poorly endowed with commercially valuable mineral resources than any other region in the country.

From an economic point of view, the mineral resources of an area may be defined as all the materials that are taken from the ground: metallic ores, non-metallic minerals, coal and oil, sand and gravel, building stone, and crushed rock. It is true that Vermont produces such non-metallic minerals as talc, asbestos, and building stones such as marble, slate, and granite; yet the entire mineral production of this state accounts for only about one-tenth of one percent of the total yearly value of the nation's mineral production. The rest of the New England states have even less valuable resources; practically the only materials of any commercial value in the rest of the region are sand, gravel, and crushed rock used for highway building and other construction. The entire yearly mineral output of New England amounts to only four-tenths of one percent of the nation's total mineral production. Put another way, for every hundred dollars that the nation earns from materials dug from the earth, New England contributes only 40 cents.

This is not to say that economically valuable metallic minerals never have been found here. The list of those found within the six-state region is almost as long as from any other region in the country, but New England's metallic minerals invariably occur in such miniscule quantities as to make profitable recovery practically impossible. For example, iron, copper, tin, lead, uranium, zinc, tungsten, manganese, even gold and silver, as well as a long list of rare metals, are all found here, but almost never in paying quantities. What commercially valuable deposits did occur in New England were mostly exhausted in the eighteenth and nineteenth centuries; few of these could ever have competed with the richer ore bodies opened up later in the west.

There were large copper mines at Ely, Vermont, and Blue Hill, Maine. In fact, in the 1870s, at the height of its production, the Ely Mine was the largest copper producer in the United States, but the fabulous copper deposits of Michigan quickly eclipsed Ely's production. Recent exploration in the Blue Hill area in Maine has disclosed some low-grade copper ore which might be developed in the future.

Most of the other metallic ores have had similar histories. Iron was mined at Bennington, Vermont; Monson, Maine; and Roxbury, Connecticut. Tungsten came from Trumbull, Connecticut; lead was found near Loudville and Leverett, Massachusetts; tin was mined near Paris, Maine; and so on down the list.

Many New England towns can boast of "gold" or "silver" mines. Many of these were merely holes blasted in the gray country rock by a farmer seeking greater fortune than he was able to glean from the thin soil. Others were elaborate stock swindles that yielded nothing but fool's gold— and perhaps a fortune for their operators through the sale of bogus stock certificates. A small minority of New England gold and silver mines actually did yield a little ore; most did not.

Many of these little mines are far richer in local color than they ever were in ore. Many have histories of odd intrigues, eccentric people, high hopes, and bitter disappointment. And many of the older residents in the towns, always a valuable source of local history, can supply anecdotes about these old mines.

It is still possible to find gold in Maine. The Swift

River north of Rumford has gold in its gravels. Nowhere is it plentiful, but the region around Byron seems to be the most productive. Although the gold is too scarce for commercial exploitation, a few people made a living of sorts panning gold during the Depression. Hard work will still yield small quantities. Many people have searched in vain for the "mother lode," the source of the Swift River gold. It is doubtful if any lode actually exists, or, if one does exist, it is probably deeply buried.

The fossil fuels, coal and oil, have also largely passed New England by. No oil has been found within the region's boundaries, nor is it likely to be. The rocks are too old and too highly metamorphosed. There is a possibility, however, of finding oil in the younger sediments that lie submerged off New England's coast.

New England is only slightly better endowed with coal. One small commercial coal field exists in Rhode Island's Narragansett Basin near Kingston; coal deposits of potential economic value may exist near Mansfield, Massachusetts. Elsewhere, it is a geological curiosity. Lignite, a low grade variety of coal, occurs at the base of Gay Head Cliffs at Martha's Vineyard and in a clay pit at Brandon, Vermont. There is also coal in the Triassic rocks in the Massachusetts end of the Connecticut Lowland, but here as elsewhere the seams are far too thin to mine. When one views the desolation and ugliness in other parts of the country caused by coal mining, perhaps this lack of coal in New England is more an asset than a liability.

Places to Visit:

There are no metal mines presently in operation in New England. Few if any of the now abandoned mines produced any of the spectacular mineral specimens found in some of the western mines. It is still possible, though, to find specimens of common minerals on the dumps of the abandoned mines. Many of these mines, together with the minerals reported from them and directions for reaching them, are listed in the following bibliography.

Swift River, Byron, Maine (USGS Rumford). It is still possible to pan gold in the river.

Books to Read:

Maine Metal Mines and Prospects by Arthur M. Hussey II, 1958 (available from Maine Department of Economic Development, 85¢ plus tax). A booklet listing all known metal mines and prospects in the state and minerals reputed to have been found in each. Maps for reaching the locations are included. (Out of Print)

The Geology of New Hampshire: Part III, Minerals and Mines by T. R. Meyers and Glenn W. Stewart, 1956 (available from the New Hampshire Dept. of Resources and Economic Development, $1.50). A list of all the mineral locations in the state. (Out of Print)

Connecticut Minerals, Their Properties and Occurrence, Bulletin 77, by Julian A. Sohon (Connecticut Geological and Natural History Survey). A description of the minerals found in Connecticut and a list of towns and the minerals found in each. (Available from the State Librarian, $2.00.)

Mineral Deposits and Occurrences in Connecticut, Map MR7, by Nancy C. Pearre (Connecticut Geological and Natural History Survey). A map showing the locations of the various mining areas in the state. (Available from the State Librarian, 50¢.)

Economic Geology of Massachusetts ed. by O. C. Farquar, 1968 (available from the University of Massachusetts,

$5.00). A collection of papers on Massachusetts geology delivered at a conference in 1967. Section on the "mineral belt" in the Berkshire Hills listing location of mines.

Maine Mines and Mineral Locations: Vol. II, Eastern Maine and New Hampshire Mines and Mineral Locations by Philip Morrill, 1957 (both are available from Winthrop Mineral Shop, P.O. Box 105, E. Winthrop, Me. 04343). List of mines by towns, and minerals found in each. Maps showing mine locations.

Vermont Mines and Mineral Locations, Vols. I and II, by Philip Morrill, 1958 (available from Dartmouth College Museum, Hanover, N.H., $1.00 each). Similar lists of Vermont mineral locations.

Placer Gold in Maine (available from Maine Department of Economic Development free of charge). Mimeographed sheet of gold panning localities in Maine.

Mineral Collecting in Vermont by Raymond W. Grant (Vermont Geological Survey special publication no. 2, Montpelier, Vt.). Well-illustrated guide to mineral collecting localities in the state. Excellent for amateurs.

Rockhound's Guide to Connecticut by Kathleen H. Ryerson (Pequot 1972) descriptions with maps of the important mineral collecting sites in Connecticut. Excellent for amateurs.

New England Pegmatites

No matter how scanty its metallic mineral resources, many mineral collectors consider New England a treasurehouse. Their opinion is almost entirely based on the existence of another also largely defunct mineral industry, pegmatite mining. In composition pegmatite resembles granite; the main constituents of both are usually quartz, feldspar, and mica, with smaller amounts of other minerals. The main difference between the two types of rock is in the size of the individual crystallized grains of these constituent minerals. In granite they are usually only a fraction of an inch in diameter; in pegmatite they may range up to several feet or more. In pegmatites these minerals are often commercially valuable because they occur in large enough masses to make hand separation possible.

Most of the pegmatite mines were worked primarily for feldspar, a white mineral that has found use in the manufacture of fine porcelain and scouring powder. Pegmatites containing large plates of mica have been even more valuable since mica has had many uses, ranging from the windows in old-fashioned cook stoves to parts of modern electronic equipment. Clear quartz has been used in optical equipment and abrasives. Recently beryl, one of the minor constituent minerals in pegmatite, has been mined as an ore of beryllium, a light metal used in alloys. Several pegmatite mines have produced a number of other valuable minerals as well.

Pegmatite, having essentially the same composition as granite, is usually associated with large granite bodies. It often occurs as coarse-grained masses within the granite or as dikes or pod-shaped pipes leading from the granite out into the surrounding rock. Pegmatites were probably formed at great depths, the feldspar, quartz, and some of the other minerals crystallizing out of a thick molten fluid. Geologists believe that most of the New England pegmatites were formed at the same time as the granites.

Most of New England's pegmatite mines have been small open pits. Some of these have been extended underground, but only a few mines in New Hampshire have been worked primarily as underground operations

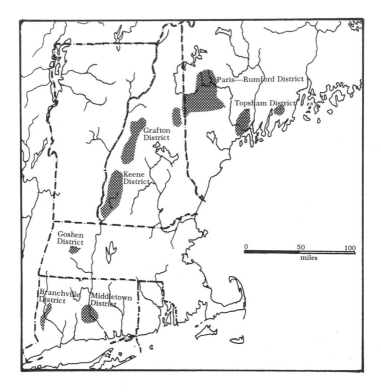

Map of southern New England showing the major pegmatite districts (after Cameron).

with vertical shafts and tunnels. Since the majority of the commercially valuable deposits have been small in size, mining operations were correspondingly small-scale. Usually a crew of about a half dozen men worked a mine, blasting the rock loose and separating the various minerals by hand. Almost all of the mines have had histories of intermittent operation, reflecting the fluctuations in prices for their minerals.

Mining began during the 1800s and reached its high-water mark during World War II when prices for strategic minerals were high. Since then the industry has languished; mineral prices are lower, competition from imports has increased, and most of the high grade New England pegmatites have been exhausted. Nevertheless, the total output of these little mines has been impressive: in the last century and a half they have yielded several million tons of minerals, mostly feldspar.

What makes some of these mines so interesting to mineral collectors is the large number of additional minerals, many of them rare, that are uncovered during mining operations. A number of mines have also produced splendid semi-precious gem-stones. The gems and exotic minerals are almost wholly confined to pegmatite bodies that have undergone secondary mineralization. In these, hot mineral-bearing solutions have bubbled up through the rock, eating cavities in it and depositing crystals of gems and rare minerals in these cavities.

Out of the hundreds of known pegmatite bodies in New England, only about 50 have undergone secondary mineralization. These 50 have produced practically all of the rare minerals and most of the gems for which the region is famous. The rest are simple pegmatites, usually containing only a dozen or so relatively common minerals.

Of the number of well-known pegmatite mines in New England, perhaps the most famous is the Mt. Mica

tourmaline mine near Paris, Maine. In 1845, two boys discovered the deposit when they found an emerald-green tourmaline crystal shining in the roots of an overturned tree. The first snow of the winter fell that very night, but in the following spring, they discovered several "gem pockets," large solution cavities lined with tourmaline crystals, and mining operations began in earnest.

Mt. Mica produced some of New England's finest gemstones — clear tourmaline crystals, large and small, in colors across the whole spectrum. Some of the most striking were the watermelon tourmalines, clear gem crystals with a deep pink core and an exterior of green. Other were banded, first green or blue, then pink, then green again. The collection at Harvard's Peabody Museum houses many Mt. Mica tourmalines, including the largest crystal ever found there, a giant weighing several pounds. One of the treasures of the Peabody was the Hamlin Necklace, a priceless collection of cut Mt. Mica tourmalines of every color mounted in a gold necklace. In 1961 the necklace was stolen; it has never been recovered.

Mt. Mica is one New England pegmatite mine that has not been exhausted; there are probably many more magnificent tourmaline crystals still lying undiscovered in the pegmatite. Their recovery is problematic, however, for the narrow gem zone slopes downward under an increasingly thick layer of barren rock that must first be removed. As a result, mining becomes more and more costly. Recently one section of the mine was reopened on a small scale and yielded several pockets of splendid crystals.

Several other mines in Maine bear mentioning. The Newry Mines near Rumford have yielded 65 minerals including colorful watermelon tourmalines up to five inches in diameter. Most of these were not of gem

Mica mine, North Waterford, Maine. Many of these small pegmatite mines have produced gemstones and rare minerals as by-products. Most are now abandoned.

quality, however, since they occurred not in pockets but in a quartz matrix that shattered and cracked during mining. The Black Mountain Mica Mine, also in the Rumford area, produced beautiful specimens of pink tourmaline as well as a large number of other minerals. Mt. Apatite, near Auburn, is famous for its gem tourmalines and several other striking minerals. In Topsham, the Fisher Quarry was one of the largest pegmatite mines in the United States, producing 17,000 tons of feldspar in a single year. Here were found some pockets of magnificent blue topaz. The Bumpus Quarry in Albany has produced some excellent blue beryl crystals, including a single crystal 25 feet long, as well as tons of rose quartz.

The Harvard Mine in Greenwood is another well-known pegmatite mine. Harvard University worked the mine in 1924 for mineral specimens. The rock of this mine is another good example of a compound pegmatite; it is full of crystal-lined cavities illustrating secondary mineralization. The mine has yielded over 25 different minerals, several of them rare and many in splendid crystal groups.

New Hampshire has had its share of excellent gem and mineral localities as well. The Palermo Mine near North Groton holds the record for the greatest variety of minerals found in a New England mine. The pegmatite here has yielded 86 different minerals, including half a dozen found nowhere else in the world. Although gem tourmaline does not occur in New Hampshire, many mines have produced excellent aquamarine beryl crystals. The best have come from the Valencia Mine, the Rice Mine, and the Fletcher Mine in the North Groton area. Uranium minerals are common at many of the New England pegmatites, but only at the Ruggles Mine in Grafton do they occur in a large enough quantity to be of potential commercial value.

Several pegmatite mines in Connecticut are also interesting. The Gillette Quarry in Haddam and the Strickland Quarry in Portland have both produced gem tourmalines. These and several other Connecticut mines have yielded gem beryl of various colors, including a rare pink-to-rose-red variety. A total of 70 different minerals has been found in the quarries around Portland and Middletown, and one small mica mine near Branchville yielded 60 different minerals, including nine found for the first time.

The above list is far from complete. Within each of the main pegmatite regions there are many other mines and prospects that have produced gemstones and interesting minerals. Almost all of the mines are closed now, but mineral collectors still come to scratch the dumps or hammer at the quarry walls for specimens. Although many of these mines have been closed for years, collectors still occasionally make unusual finds. These are almost always the result of careful observation and hard work; sometimes collectors have to remove tons of rock to reach fresh material. Many of these mines are still worth visiting, but no one should expect to find many rare or valuable mineral specimens lying about.

The prognosis for New England pegmatites is not hopeful. During World War II, government geologists surveyed practically all of the major pegmatite bodies known at the time. The results of their studies showed that almost all of the existing mines were about worked out. Since then, geologists have made intensive studies of several of the more promising pegmatite areas in hopes of finding new deposits, but the results of these studies were also disappointing.

No doubt only a fraction of New England's pegmatite bodies have been discovered thus far; probably many more deposits, potentially valuable for both mine operators and mineral collectors alike, still lie buried beneath the mantle of glacial debris that covers the bedrock. Perhaps some new prospecting method will be devised to locate these hidden deposits. But in the meantime, each year brings a larger number of collectors to the abandoned mines in search of specimens. It has been the large variety of minerals found in the pegmatite bodies, more than anything else, that has given New England a reputation for great mineral wealth.

Places to Visit:

There are dozens of interesting pegmatite mines in New England. People with any serious interest in exploring these old mines should buy one of the inexpensive guides listed in the following bibliography. Space does not permit detailed directions to the mines mentioned in the text other than their general location in the townships. Inquire locally for directions.

Mt. Mica, Paris, Maine (USGS Buckfield). One and one-half miles northeast of village of Paris Hill. Old gem workings on hilltop; mine dumps scattered through woods behind mine.

Newry Mine, Newry, Maine (USGS Rumford). Mine is one mile off Route 5 near northwest corner of Rumford. There are several mines and prospects on hill. Tourmaline mine on top of hill. Feldspar mine that produced many specimens of rare minerals. Large workings about three-quarters of the way up.

Black Mountain Mica Mines, Rumford, Maine (USGS Rumford). Mine about 5 miles northwest of town.

Mt. Apatite Mines, Auburn, Maine (USGS Poland). Mines located on hilltop three-quarters of a mile north of Haskells Corner.

Topsham Mines, Topsham, Maine (USGS Bath). Fisher Quarry, one of dozens of mines on low ridge northeast of the town. These mines, as a group, have not been as rich a source of mineral specimens as have some others.

Bumpus Quarry, Albany, Maine (USGS Bethel). Route 5, one mile south of Albany Town House.

Harvard Mine, Greenwood, Maine (USGS Bryant Pond). About 8 miles northwest of Norway, Maine.

North Groton area, N.H. (USGS Cardigan). Palermo and Rice Mines on hill about one and one-half miles west of village; Fletcher and Valencia mines about 3 miles east of village.

Ruggles Mine, Grafton, N.H. (USGS Cardigan). About 2 miles southwest of village.

Strickland Quarry, Portland, Conn. (USGS Middle Haddam). Two miles south of village. Largest of several interesting Pegmatite Mines in the Portland-Middletown area.

Peabody Museum, Harvard University, Cambridge, Mass. Contains what is probably the best collection of New England minerals in the U.S. Examining labeled specimens of the various minerals is one of the easiest ways to learn them.

American Museum of Natural History, Central Park West at 79th Street, New York City, has a large suite of New England pegmatites.

Books to Read:
(See also books listed on pages 65–66)

Maine Pegmatite Mines and Prospects and Associated Minerals by John R. Rand, 1957 (Maine Department of

Economic Development, 50¢ plus tax). Listing of the mines, location, and minerals reported from each. Mines and prospects are located on maps. Very comprehensive listing.

Maine Mines and Mineral Locations: Vol. I, Western Maine by Philip Morrill, 1956 (available from Winthrop Mineral Shop, P.O. Box 105, East Winthrop, Maine, $2.95). Listing of mines and prospects together with minerals found in each by township. Comprehensive.

The Geology of New Hampshire: Part III, Minerals and Mines by T. R. Meyers and Glenn W. Stewart (described on page 65). (Out of Print)

Connecticut Minerals, Their Properties and Occurrence by Julian A. Sohon (described on page 65).

Beryl Resources of New Hampshire, U.S. Geological Survey Professional Paper 353, by James J. Page and David M. Larrabee (available from U.S. Government Printing Office).

General Books on Minerals and Mineral Collecting:

Getting Acquainted with Minerals by G. L. English and D. E. Jensen (McGraw Hill, 1959). An excellent beginning text. (Out of Print)

Minerals and How to Study Them by E. S. Dana & C. S. Hurlburt (Wiley, 1949). Another excellent beginning text.

Gemstones and Minerals, How and Where to Find Them by John Sinkankas (Van Nostrand, 1961). A wealth of practical information about prospecting and mineral collecting. Large section on pegmatites. (Out of Print)

A boulder-strewn pasture, Princeton, Massachusetts. New England's rocky soil is one of the main reasons why there is little farming in the region.

Part II
The Face of the Land

Much of New England superficially resembles the Piedmont region, the upland area of the Middle Atlantic States lying between the coastal plain and the Blue Ridge Mountains. Both regions are hilly, both have bedrock relatively near the surface, both have many rivers and streams flowing across them, and both regions will become wooded if the land is left undisturbed.

Yet, on closer examination, a number of differences between the two regions are apparent. The natural lakes so common in New England are almost entirely absent in the Piedmont. Absent also are the extensive areas of bog and swampland. The boulders strewn about the New England countryside are confined in the Piedmont only to the stream bottoms. The large areas of exposed ledge common to most New England hills are only found here and there on the Piedmont Valley sides.

The soils of the two regions are different as well. In the Piedmont, roadcuts and other excavations often reveal a reddish yellow soil profile in which the topsoil grades imperceptibly through layers of decayed and broken rock fragments into the solid bedrock below. This type of profile indicates that, as a result of millions of years of weathering, the topsoil and mantle rock have come directly from the underlying bedrock.

Much of New England's subsoil is *till*, an unsorted mixture of clay, sand, and broken rock. The rocks in this mixture are usually of several different types, some having traveled many miles from their parent outcrops. In addition, most of the bedrock surfaces beneath the till are smooth and fresh, showing none of the weathering and decay on the upper layers that is characteristic to the south. The rocky layer of till is one of the main reasons why much of New England is not fit for cultivation.

Until quite recently — by the measure of geologic time — New England's landscape probably closely resembled that of the Piedmont. Then, one after another, at least four and possibly sixteen huge sheets of ice pushed southward from what is now Canada. These ice sheets, though not powerful enough to level the already existing hills and mountains, did cause drastic changes in the face of the land. The slowly moving ice churned rocks and soil together into the jumbled layer of till that now covers so much of the land; it cleaned the bedrock of its soil cover; and its debris clogged valleys, dammed the streams, and produced the familiar lakes, large areas of swampland, and waterfalls—all uncommon features in regions not touched by the ice.

These glacial invasions caused many other changes in the landscape, changes that baffled early geologists for

Banking of glacial till, Otter Creek, Maine. Most of the boulders are of granite, the local bedrock.

decades until they realized that a sheet of ice, not Noah's flood, was the key to explaining the landscape. We have examined the part that New England's bedrock framework played in the evolution of the present day landscape. In the following sections we shall turn our attention to the ice sheets and the profound changes they wrought upon the face of the land.

Close-up of till lying on bedrock, Arlington, Massachusetts. The contact with the underlying bedrock is fresh and distinct. Note the angular pieces of bedrock in the clayey till.

The Birth of an Ice Sheet

When we pick up a handful of snow and pack it into a snowball, we are repeating — on a tiny scale — the process that gives birth to a glacier. Snow is the raw material of glaciers. That light, fluffy snow could spawn these enormously destructive rivers of ice may seem hard to believe at first, but the snowball in our hands is the evidence. When we squeeze a handful of snow together we cause the tiny, delicate snow crystals to fuse together into a hard, heavy snowball; where snow is deep, its weight alone will compact the lower layers, accomplishing the same thing. If we had a strong enough grip and could continue to squeeze our snowball for a long enough time, we would continue to pack the snow crystals ever more tightly together until our snowball turned to ice; likewise the continuous pressure of a really high pile of snow will eventually turn the packed snow on the bottom of the pile into solid ice. The weight of a snow bank a few tens of feet high will provide enough pressure to cause this change.

If snow continues to fall and the accumulation reaches a depth of 100 to 200 feet, the lower layers, although solid ice, assume the character of a thick liquid, which can no longer support the weight of the snow and ice above, and the whole mass begins to move. When this happens, a glacier is born.

Like most other geological processes, the growth of a glacier is slow. There is no place on earth where enough snow falls in a single year to build and sustain a glacier. Melting and evaporation take place even on Greenland and Antarctica. The only prerequisite for a glacier is that more snow falls over the years than melts or evaporates. When this occurs, the snow eventually piles up until it reaches the depth for glacial movement to begin.

Climate, then, is an obvious determining factor in glacial birth and growth. For glaciers to grow there must be a drop in average yearly temperature or an increase in snowfall or both. A lower average summer temperature seems particularly crucial; there are many regions in the world today which experience sufficiently heavy winter snowfalls to produce glaciers if only slightly cooler summer temperatures prevailed.

About one million years ago there was a slight, but perhaps worldwide, change in the climate. Measured by human lifetimes, the change was probably imperceptible, perhaps taking several thousand years to complete. Nevertheless, this climatic change was enough to start a chain of events which has not yet come to an end. One of the places that experienced a cooler climate with increased snowfall was the Laurentian Uplands in northeastern Canada. The Laurentians may already have been receiving fairly heavy winter snowfalls, and a drop in the average summer temperature of only a few degrees was enough to cause snow on the high ground to linger through the summer. As the centuries passed, the snowfields grew, one coalescing with another until large upland areas lay buried. Tongues of glacial ice began creeping down the valleys. The snow continued to accumulate and the glaciers increased in size until finally, many thousands of years later, the whole Laurentian Uplands lay buried beneath an unbroken layer of ice, probably not unlike the present-day Greenland Icecap. As the snow continued to fall in the Uplands, the glacial ice began to spread in all directions: northward toward the cold Arctic, westward toward the drier interior, eastward toward the Atlantic and southward toward New England.

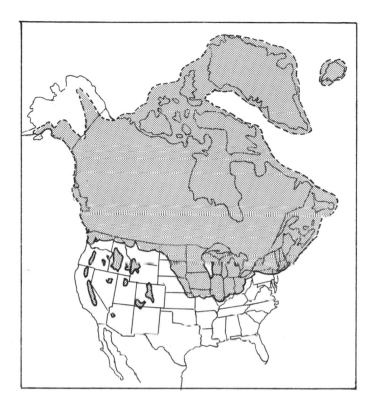

Map of North America showing extent of Pleistocene glaciation (after Flint).

Probably it took thousands of years for the Laurentide ice sheet to reach New England. Even at its fastest, glacial movement can be reckoned in only feet per day. In addition, there may have been minor climatic fluctuations which slowed or even stopped the glacial advance for a time. Yet, as the years passed, the glacier pushed slowly across the St. Lawrence Valley and southward across New England until the whole region lay buried under a thick sheet of ice.

At first the ice chose the easiest paths southward, creeping down the already existing river valleys. Gradually, however, the ice tongues thickened and deepened until only the higher mountain peaks remained as scattered islands above a cold white sea of ice. The glacier continued to thicken until even the highest peaks finally disappeared beneath the icy onslaught.

Books to Read:

The World of Ice by James L. Dyson (Knopf, 1963). A clear, readable account of glaciers. The emphasis is on mountain glaciation areas where glaciers are still active, and the book provides a close look at the types of evidence which have led geologists to reconstruct the events of the Ice Age. Excellent photographs.

Glacial and Pleistocene Geology by Richard F. Flint (Wiley, 1957). Standard college text by one of America's foremost authorities on glacial geology. Appropriate for any serious student. (Out of Print)

The Quarternary of the United States ed. by H. E. Wright and D. G. Frey (Princeton, 1964). A comprehensive review of the state of knowledge about all aspects of this most recent period in the long history of the earth. Technical but of great value to serious students of the Ice Age.

Glaciers and the Ice Age by Gwen Schultz (Holt, 1963). An account of the Ice Age for laymen. Emphasis on early man.

Glacial Scour

About a hundred years ago, when the idea of an ice age first gained acceptance, many people envisioned the overriding ice sheets as having reduced New England's mountains from alpine proportions to their modest present-day height. This was not the case. Before the ice sheet, the mountains were probably approximately the same height as they are today. Although the ice did shape them somewhat and did remove the accumulation of residual soil and broken mantle rock produced by years of weathering, it scraped off, on the average, only a relatively small amount of the solid bedrock below.

Solid rock is harder than ice. The tough granites and schists of the mountains had resisted the slow but constant forces of erosion and weathering for perhaps a million years prior to glaciation; they resisted almost equally well the ravages of the four glacial onslaughts.

New England's familiar granite quarries have provided us with some measure of the extent of glacial erosion. Granite ledges are split by a series of *joints,* parallel cracks, running in various directions. The joints that run parallel to the surface, known in quarry terminology as the *sheet joints,* exhibit the characteristic of being closer together near the surface and becoming increasingly farther apart deeper in the ledge. Moreover, the distance between the joints increases at a rate that is proportional to the depth.

By comparing the distance between the highest sheet joints in New England ledges to the more closely spaced joints near the surface of unglaciated ledges to the south, it is possible to get a rough measurement of how much bedrock has been scoured away. The results show surprisingly small amounts. In the central New England quarries that were investigated, it was found that the glacier removed only 10 or 15 feet of the bedrock on top of the ledges. Granite, however, is among the toughest of rocks; probably glacial ice has been more erosive in areas of softer bedrock.

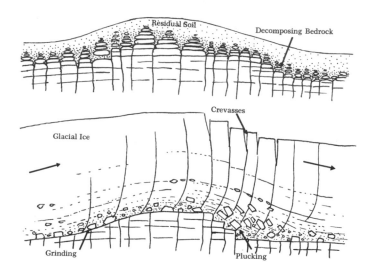

Three cross-sectional diagrams showing glacial erosion on a small bedrock hill. Note the asymmetric stoss and lee topography in the lower diagram. Many of New England's larger hills and mountains illustrate this same asymmetric shape (after Sharp).

Boulders and debris frozen in the glacial ice acted like sandpaper as they rode across the bedrock below. Rock upon rock slowly grinding against each other produced a fine dust, aptly called *rock flour*. In areas of softer bedrock the rock flour gives glacial till a sticky, clay-like consistency.

Although its erosive force was relatively weak on the tops of the hills, as the ice moved down the other side it had a much more pronounced effect. Instead of merely scouring the bedrock as it rode down on the lee slopes of hills, the ice plucked loose larger blocks of bedrock and carried them away. This continual plucking away of bedrock gave the hills a curious asymmetric profile — gradual north or *stoss slopes* and steep south or *lee slopes*. The bedrock broke along the joint planes which were opened by freezing meltwater that had seeped into them. The sheet joint studies quoted earlier have shown that as much as 100 feet of bedrock on the southern sides of granite hills has been removed in this manner.

Where the ice flow concentrated into a fairly narrow area as it did in the valleys of the White Mountains, the glaciers did a spectacular carving job. The high mountains on either side funneled the ice into the valleys and caused it to abrade the valley walls and floors to a much greater degree than it could abrade the bedrock across the open country.

As the great fingers of ice thrust southward down the mountain valleys, they removed all the loose rock which had been tumbling off the mountains for millions of years and ground away at the solid bedrock floors beneath. Glaciated valleys usually have rounded floors. Where glacial scour has been intense the valleys exhibit a characteristic U-shape cross section with steep side-walls. In New England perhaps as much as 500 feet of bedrock was scoured out of the deepest valleys.

Even when the ice reached such a thickness that it was able to pass over the mountain peaks, the lower layers of the ice continued to follow the valleys, even when they greatly diverged from the general direction of the ice flow. The major White Mountain notches — Crawford, Franconia, Pinkham, and Dixville in New

Crawford Notch, New Hampshire. The U-shaped valley floor is the result of glacial scour.

Hampshire; Hazen's Notch in Vermont; and the north-south valleys in the Katahdin and Bar Harbor regions in Maine — all have characteristic rounded floors caused by glacial scour. In addition, many of the higher mountain passes and the "saddles" between the peaks, enlarged when the glacial ice finally piled up high enough

to spill through them, also exhibit the same U-shaped profiles.

In Franconia Notch, late in the day, the low sun brings out long horizontal gouges in the smooth valley sidewalls where the streams of ice dragged boulders along them. Gouges and scratches produced by boulders under tons of moving ice are not restricted merely to the mountain valleys but may be seen on bedrock ledges all across New England. At one time, probably soon after the final ice melted, it might have been possible to see scratches on practically every exposed ledge, but now, several thousands of years later, weathering has obliterated most of these marks. Glacial scratches can still be seen on most fresh bedrock surfaces wherever the overlying till has recently been stripped away.

Glacial scratches on ledge, Mt. Desert Island, Maine. Scratches were made by rocks dragged along under the moving ice.

These glacial scratches have been valuable indicators of glacial movement. From them and from the asymmetric stoss and lee topography discussed earlier, and from other evidence which we will presently examine, it has been possible to determine the general direction of the ice movement across New England. The wide variation in the direction of the glacial scratches in the valleys from those higher on the mountains has given some indication of how the local topography deflected the ice from its general southeastern course.

Some of New England's most striking scenery was created by smaller glaciers that flowed down the higher mountainsides just prior to the arrival of the continental ice sheet and, in some places, just after it melted away. These glaciers transformed small, pre-glacial mountain valleys into spectacular basins called *cirques*.

The steep-sided, bowl-shaped cirques were formed when meltwater seeped into the bedrock joints and froze, loosening large blocks. The moving ice carried these away rather than allowing them to accumulate on the valley floors as piles of talus.

In the White Mountains, there are about a dozen well-developed glacial cirques and a number of smaller valleys which appear to have undergone some mountain glaciation. Of these, Tuckerman's Ravine on the east side of Mt. Washington is the best known. Here a mountain glacier carved a symmetrical, rounded glacial trough about 800 feet deep and a third of a mile wide. Other spectacular glacial valleys in the Presidential Range include Huntington Ravine and Great Gulf. Even today, snow lasts in these ravines until mid-June and gives ski enthusiasts an extra month or two of spring skiing. A drop in average summer temperature of only 10 degrees and a little heavier yearly snowfall could probably reestablish glaciers there.

Tuckerman's Ravine, Mt. Washington, New Hampshire. A small glacier on the eastern flank of Mt. Washington produced this spectacular, bowl-like cirque.

The Mt. Katahdin region in central Maine has seven well-developed cirques. The largest of these, Great Basin, on Katahdin's east flank, is regarded by many to be the best example of mountain glaciation in the eastern United States. From Chimney Pond, lying on the scooped-out basin floor, steep headwalls ring the cirque like an immense horseshoe, leaving only a trough-like exit on the northeast side.

One of the mountain glaciers that grew in this basin cut back nearly to Katahdin's summit, carving an almost vertical headwall 2,000 feet high. On the south side of the summit this glacier cut all the way through the mountain flank, forming a knife-like ridge with Katahdin's steep south side. This sharp ridge, aptly called the "Knife Edge," is so narrow in places that it is possible to stand astride it, one foot on the headwall and the other on Katahdin's southern slope.

A good part of the Great Basin lies above the timberline. The rock is fresh and unweathered, suggesting that glacial ice left the region more recently than it did the White Mountains. This may well be the case. In fact, a long crescent-shaped mound of boulders lying near the basin's headwall may still be covering a last remnant of the mountain glacier which carved it.

About a mile down the valley from Chimney Pond, a long ridge of boulders has dammed the mountain streams, forming a series of ponds. The boulders in this ridge are of the same granite found in the walls of Great Basin and were undoubtedly torn loose and carried there by the glacier which flowed out of the basin. This ridge of glacial debris, called a *moraine*, marks the meeting place of the Great Basin mountain glacier with the long streams of continental ice, by then reduced in thickness but still actively moving. The larger ice flow deflected the Great Basin glacier southward, leaving a long trail of boulders where the two met. During the height of

Knife Edge, Mt. Katahdin, Maine. The sharp ridge was formed where a glacial cirque, to the left, has intersected Katahdin's southern slope.

glaciation, the continental ice sheet rode over Mt. Katahdin; had the moraine been formed prior to this time, it probably would have been destroyed.

Although it is not yet known how many years ago glacial activity on Katahdin finally ceased, this moraine is fairly conclusive evidence that mountain glaciers existed here after the continental ice sheet had begun to wane. Such evidence is lacking in the White Mountains and elsewhere in New England.

Places to Visit:

Franconia Notch, U.S. Route 3 (USGS Franconia). Striking U-shaped glacial valley.

Crawford Notch, U.S. Route 302 (USGS Crawford Notch). Another classic example of a glaciated valley.

Evans Notch, Route 113, Gilead, Maine (USGS Bethel).

Kinsman Notch, Route 112, Woodstock, N.H. (USGS Moosilauke).

Dixville Notch, Route 26, Dixville, N.H. (USGS Dixville).

Pinkham Notch, Route 16, south of Gorham, N.H. (USGS Gorham).

Grafton Notch, Route 26, Grafton, Maine (USGS Old Speck). The ascent up Old Speck Mountain west of notch is steepest climb along Appalachian Trail.

Hazen's Notch, Montgomery Center, Vermont, Route 58 (USGS Jay Peak).

Acadia National Park, Mt. Desert Island, Maine (USGS Mt. Desert). Most of the north-south valleys on Mt. Desert Island illustrate a U-shaped profile.

Glacial Cirques on Presidential Range (USGS Mt. Washington):

Tuckerman's Ravine, east side of Mt. Washington, visible from Route 16 north of Pinkham Notch. One of the main trails up Mt. Washington climbs the ravine.

Huntington Ravine, east side of Mt. Washington, about a mile north of Tuckerman's Ravine. A smaller but very sharp-sided cirque. The trail to the summit up Huntington Ravine is the steepest ascent on the mountain.

Great Gulf, a huge cirque on the north side of Mt. Washington, visible from both the carriage road and the cog railway. Two smaller mountain glaciers on the side of Mt. Jefferson also fed into this valley.

King's Ravine, north side of Mt. Adams, visible from Route 2 west of Gorham. Two trails ascend King's Ravine.

Ravine of the Castles, north side of Mt. Jefferson, near Kinsman.

Jobildunk Ravine (USGS Moosilauke), north side of Mt. Moosilauke.

Glacial Cirques on Mt. Katahdin (USGS Katahdin), north and east sides of mountain:

Great Basin, see description in text. Accessible from Chimney Pond Trail from Roaring Brook campsite.

South Basin, adjacent to Great Basin. Headwall forms Knife Edge. Cathedral Trail ascends the steep spur between the two basins.

North Basin, spectacular cirque one mile north of Great Basin. Accessible from Chimney Pond.

Several other glacial cirques on northern end of mountain.

Glacial Cirques in Sugarloaf Region (USGS Bigelow), several smaller glacial cirques on mountains north of Kingfield, Maine.

Basin Pond Moraine (USGS Mt. Katahdin), east side of mountain accessible from Chimney Pond Trail. Only evidence of mountain glaciation during late glacial times in New England. See description in text.

Books to Read:

The Geology of New Hampshire: Part I, Surficial Geology by J. W., L., & K. P. Goldthwait, 1951 (available from New Hampshire Dept. of Resources and Economic Development). Discusses all aspects of New Hampshire's glacial geology in layman's terms. Large-scale map of glacial features included. (Out of Print)

The Geology of Baxter State Park by D. W. Caldwell, 1960 (available from Maine Dept. of Economic Development, or from Park Headquarters, Millinocket, 75¢). Layman's discussion of both bedrock and glacial geology of Katahdin region.

Katahdin 1966 ed. by D. W. Caldwell (New England Intercollegiate Geological Conference). Guide to both bedrock and glacial geology of Katahdin Region. Presupposes some geological knowledge. A series of field trips arranged and trip log with mileages along routes. (Out of Print)

A.M.C. Guide to Country Walks Near Boston by Alan Fisher. 1977 (available from Appalachian Mountain Club, $4.95). Interpretive guidebook to natural areas within reach of public transportation.

Glacial Boulders

Boulders are almost as common on New England hill-sides as the pines and birches that grow there. Not only did the ice sheet plane away almost all the soil that had been slowly forming on these hills, but it dislodged some of the solid bedrock as well. In some places the ice tore large blocks loose and dragged them along; these loose pieces of rock became the boulders now scattered across the New England countryside.

Some parts of New England seem to have received far more than their share of boulders. One such place was Cape Ann, Massachusetts. In 1835, Edward Hitchcock, one of the pioneers of American geology, believed that the barren, rock-strewn pastures of Cape Ann must have resembled the landscape that greeted Noah when the floodwaters receded. Although much of Cape Ann has returned to woods since Hitchcock's time, its boulders are still impressive. Many other places at least approaching the rockiness of Cape Ann may be found elsewhere in New England.

It is the bedrock itself, not some whim of the glacier, that provided Cape Ann and other rocky places with a great abundance of boulders. Areas underlain by granite or other hard bedrock usually have large numbers of boulders scattered about the surface. Anyone who has attacked a piece of granite with a hammer knows how it resists being broken, but ledges of granite and other hard rocks will come apart relatively easily along the natural cracks or joints that are always present. When the ice rode over a ledge of hard rock it broke off blocks along these joints rather than crumbling the rock into small fragments. When the cracks were widely spaced, the resulting boulders were huge. A soft, easily breakable rock such as slate would usually be ground to clay rather than be broken into big blocks. Glacial boulders of soft rock such as slate are rare indeed.

People are often fascinated by *glacial erratics,* those boulders carried many miles by the ice and set down in a region of different bedrock. Actually, long journeys by large boulders are the exception rather than the rule. The ice dragged most large boulders for only a few miles at best; often the distance they moved could be more accurately measured in feet. Thus, the boulders in most rocky places came from the nearby ledges. Of course, smaller rocks locked in the glacial ice often traveled a hundred miles or more.

For many years geologists debated whether the ice sheet overspread New England's highest mountains or left them as isolated, unglaciated islands. Normally this would seem to be easy to determine, but on the treeless mountain summits, the harsh climate has so shattered and weathered the bedrock that almost all evidence of glaciation has been destroyed. It was the discovery of small glacial erratics — rocks differing in composition from the bedrock of the summits — on all of the high mountains that finally settled the question.

Hitchcock and other early geologists believed erratic boulders to be evidence of Noah's flood. The flood theory became more complicated by the discovery that the boulders invariably lay to the south or southeast of their parent ledges. From this evidence, geologists conjectured that the "flood" was caused by some huge upheaval in the Arctic Ocean that sent its waters rushing southward across New England. These trains of boulders trailing off to the south of their parent ledges were actually, of course, the work of the ice sheet.

Whenever the moving ice encountered a hill or mountain, it plucked off pieces of the bedrock and moved them in the direction it was traveling. When the bedrock was of an uncommon, easily identifiable rock, geologists could accurately map the fan-shaped distribution of boulders and rocks trailing off to the south or southeast of the parent ledge. These *boulder trains* gave geologists valuable information about glacial movements.

To produce the fan-shaped boulder trains, the ice must have moved in slightly different directions during the many years that it flowed down over New England. If the ice had always traveled in the same direction, the boulders torn loose would have been strung out in a line rather than fanning out as they do. The very wide boulder train from Mt. Ascutney in southern Vermont gives some information on how the glacial ice must have moved in mountainous regions. Although the ice sheet eventually crept over the mountain tops, its lower levels were widely deflected by the mountains and tended to flow around them.

Although geologists are certain that the ice sheet did not level whole mountain ranges or carry enormous boulders for hundreds of miles, it could do an impressive moving job on occasion. In Albany, New Hampshire, it broke loose a huge rock from a ledge and dragged it 2 miles into what is now the neighboring town of Madison. The Madison Boulder holds the record for size among New England's glacial boulders and ranks with the largest in the world. The rock is 83 feet long and weighs about 5,000 tons, as much as an ocean freighter. Other large boulders worth visiting are listed at the end of this section.

When millions of boulders were picked up, moved, and set down as happened in New England, some freakish situations were bound to result. Large boulders perched precariously on bare ledges are commonplace. Some of these have come to rest in such a delicately balanced position that a person can rock them. Rocking stones are quite famous locally. Long-time residents of a

Cradle Rock, Barre, Massachusetts. The moving ice sheet tore these rocks loose from ledges some distance to the north and left them perched precariously one atop the other.

region can often point out one of these boulders nearby. The New Hampshire Geological Survey lists several towns in New Hampshire where large ones occur.

Less common than the rocking stones are boulders which have come to rest one on top of another. The most famous of these is in the town of Barre, Massachusetts. There is a smaller pair in Harvard, Massachusetts, and undoubtedly others exist elsewhere. Another interesting rock is the Bartlett Boulder near Bartlett, New Hampshire. The melting ice suspended this boulder on top of four smaller ones, giving it the appearance of a wagon body on four wheels.

The early New England pioneers tried to use the rocks they found in their fields and pastures. From the smaller ones — those they could move — they built the stone walls that are now so much a part of the New England scene. The backbreaking task of clearing the fields proved to be endless; each spring the plows would turn up more rocks.

People started leaving the hill farms as early as 1800, when it became clear that they could not scratch a living from the rocky ground. One by one they abandoned the farms that only a generation or so earlier they had hacked from the wilderness. They moved to better lands farther west or into the valley towns to work in the mills. By the 1860s the exodus from the New England hill farms had become almost a stampede. There were no takers for these abandoned farms and they quickly fell into decay. The houses and barns disappeared and fields grew up to woods. Except for the stone walls stretching for miles through the woods and an occasional gnarled old apple tree growing improbably among the pines, there is now little to indicate that much of the land was ever inhabited.

Places to Visit:

Madison Boulder (USGS Ossipee Lake), off Route 113, 3 miles north of Madison, N.H. See description in text.

Bartlett Boulder (USGS Crawford Notch), on Route 302, one mile west of Bartlett Station, N.H. See description in text. Sawyer Rock, earlier thought to be the largest glacial boulder in New England, is nearby.

Monhegan Rock (USGS Montville), north of Montville, Conn., 60 feet high, estimated weight 4,000 tons.

Cradle Rock (USGS Barre), 3 miles northwest of Barre, Mass. (see illustration in text).

Enoch Doane's Rock (USGS Orleans), Eastham, Mass. Large glacial erratic on Nauset Beach Rd., one-quarter mile east of National Seashore Visitor's Center.

Dogtown Common (USGS Gloucester), near Gloucester, Mass. Site of an early village located in the rockiest area imaginable. Cellarholes to explore. Boulders 30 feet in diameter are fairly common in this region.

Cellar holes of abandoned farms can be found in almost every town in New England. Inquire locally. Digging will often turn up interesting artifacts: old bottles, dishes, nails, coins. Watch out for abandoned wells.

Books to Read:

The Changing Face of New England by Betty Flanders Thomson (Macmillan, 1958). Out of print but available in many libraries. Chapter 2 presents an account of the settling and later abandonment of the New England hill farms.

Hidden America by Roland Wells Robbins and Evan Jones (Knopf, 1959). An interesting account of archeological digs in New England and New York. The last part of the book gives advice to amateur archeologists and points out the vast wealth of archeological sites in New England. It contains enough information to launch a person on a fascinating hobby. (Out of Print)

Drumlin, Westmoreland, New Hampshire.
See description in text.

Drumlins

We have seen that New England's mountains and higher hills are masses of bedrock covered by a thin veneer of till. In many places rain has washed away the till layer from the slopes and summits, leaving the bare bedrock exposed. We have also seen how the glacier has torn loose great blocks of the bedrock from the lee sides of the hills and mountains, leaving bare cliffs and steep rocky slopes. Even when their elevations are not high, these bedrock hills give vast areas of New England a rough, rocky appearance.

In contrast, there are several smaller areas in New England where the countryside is pleasantly rolling, where bedrock outcroppings are less common, and where few boulders appear. These are the areas where smooth, rounded *drumlins* are the hills which dominate the landscape.

Even by New England standards, drumlins are relatively small hills. The biggest are usually less than a mile long and rarely rise more than 250 feet above the land. Yet these smooth, graceful hills add much to the natural beauty of the regions in which they occur. Many are still used for pasture and orchard, their open slopes providing a welcome relief to the generally wooded New England countryside.

If we examine a topographic map or an aerial photograph showing a number of these drumlins, we notice a remarkable fact: almost all of the drumlins seem to point in the same direction. Moreover, this direction matches the direction of the glacial scratches on the bedrock. Another characteristic of drumlins is that they are composed of till containing a high percentage of clay. Occasionally one is found over a mound of bedrock, but this is probably coincidental. There is no evidence that bedrock plays any part in the formation of these hills.

Drumlins usually occur in areas underlain by bedrock that is soft and hence was easily ground to clay by the ice. Geologists, however, are still unsure of the actual mode of drumlin formation. They believe that somehow the clayey till gathered into sticky masses beneath the moving ice. Gradually the ice sheet moved over these masses, adding more till to them and moulding them into their oval streamlined shape. But many unanswered questions remain. Why, for example, are they common in Massachusetts, absent from soft-rock regions of northern New England, and rare in the extreme south? Their local distribution raises questions as well; in some areas they are the dominant feature of the landscape, while nearby they are completely absent.

Probably the most famous drumlins in America are located in the Boston area. Bunker Hill, site of the Revolutionary battle, is a drumlin. These drumlins were also some of the first to be studied by the early geologists. Now every student taking the introductory geology course in the many colleges and universities in the Boston area visits one or more of these.

Just to the north of Boston occur some of the most "perfectly" shaped drumlins in New England. Many of the larger drumlins here have an elegant oval form and are so much alike that they appear to have come from

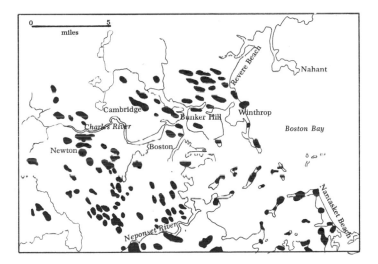

the same giant mold. On the topographic map they resemble a herd of large water animals galloping to join their companions in Boston Harbor. But the Boston drumlins are now difficult to recognize. In the last 50 years or so, the urban sprawl has crept across them one by one. In the process they have been dug away, bulldozed, built upon, and cut by highways until now their shapes are hard to see.

In addition to the Boston area, there are several other parts of New England where drumlins are common. Most occur in Massachusetts, but their distribution spills over into northeastern Connecticut and southern New Hampshire as well. They occur both as widely scattered single hills or in clusters or swarms, as they are called. Several areas where these drumlin swarms occur are listed below.

Places to Visit:

Groton, Mass. (USGS Ayer). Charming colonial town situated in a drumlin swarm.

Northern Essex County, Mass., and adjacent N.H. (USGS Newburyport West and Exeter, N.H.). Drumlin area centering around West Newbury, Mass., and Kingston, N.H. Attractive countryside.

Southern Worcester County, Mass. Many drumlins in the area to the west and south of Worcester.

World's End, Hingham, Mass. (USGS Hull & Nantasket). Entrance on Martin's Lane off Rockland St. Beautiful 249-acre peninsula into Boston Harbor. Two large drumlins. Owned by Trustees of Reservations.

A Book to Read:

Boston, A Topographical History by Walter Muir Whitehill (Harvard University Press, 1959). A fascinating account of how Boston has been built from the marshy and hilly ground into the city that we recognize today. Discusses the various drumlins in the city.

The Glacial High Water Mark

Few people studying a map of New England for the first time could fail to notice the odd shape of the land along its southern border. First, there is Cape Cod, looking like the flexed arm of an emaciated man; south of the Cape there are two roughly triangular islands, Nantucket and Martha's Vineyard; finally, a short distance to the southwest there is Long Island, somewhat resembling a fish. All of these land forms — the arm, the triangles, and the fish — owe their shape in large part to the ice sheets.

The ice sheet could not keep up its southward journey indefinitely. With each advancing mile a warmer climate was encountered. The hot sun was melting the

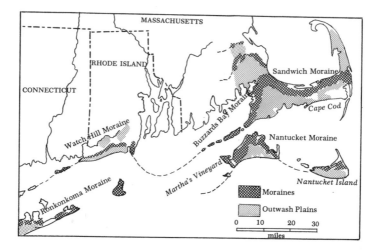

Map of southeastern New England showing moraines and outwash plains (from Glacial Map of Eastern North America, Geological Society of America).

ice, and the glacier, robbed of much of its bulk, was no longer the great shaper of hills and carver of valleys that it had been farther north. Across much of southern New England there are extensive patches of weathered till from an earlier glacial advance; evidence in the midwest clearly shows four different glacial invasions, each separated by periods of tens of thousands of years. That this weathered till still remained beneath the last glacial advance clearly shows that the ice had lost much of its erosive power.

When the ice reached a line just south of mainland New England — a line now represented by Nantucket, Martha's Vineyard, and Long Island's lower tail — its forward movement stopped entirely. Though the ice front was stationary, the glacier was not dead. Ice still slowly poured from its breeding grounds in the north carrying with it an accumulated load of boulders and debris. Like a giant conveyor belt, the ice sheet carried southward the materials that it had scraped up along the way. When it reached this southernmost line of advance — the glacial high water mark — the melting rate of the ice just equaled the glacial rate of movement and the ice front came to a standstill. As the continually moving ice melted away it dumped its rocky load and piled it up into a sinuous ridge called a *terminal moraine*. In some places the accumulation was sizable, over 200 feet high.

Although Nantucket, Martha's Vineyard, and Long Island clearly mark the farthest extent of the ice sheet to the south, little is known about how far eastward the ice had spread before coming to rest. During the time of the greatest glacial advance, the level of the sea was perhaps 200 feet lower than it is today. East and south of New England there was a gently sloping plain, a northward continuation of the coastal plain that now runs along the eastern seaboard.

As the torrents of water poured from the melting ice, they carried with them much of the finer materials, the sand and clay that the glacier had picked up en route. The sand was left spread out on top of the older marine sediments in what is known as *outwash plains;* the finer clay particles probably remained suspended in the water and were carried into the ocean.

The locations of both Nantucket and Martha's Vineyard are not mere coincidence. A study of the shapes of the moraines shows that the ice flowed in lobes rather than as a continuous single sheet. Both islands mark places where two ice lobes came together. The combined

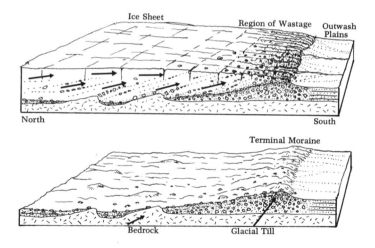

Two block diagrams showing the development of a terminal moraine. As the ice sheet moved southward it reached a point where it melted away as fast as it moved. Like a giant conveyor belt the melting ice sheet left its load of transported boulders and other glacial debris in an ever-increasing pile known as a terminal moraine (after Strahler).

debris from both lobes was higher than along the edge of a single lobe, hence the meeting points of the lobes remained as islands when the level of the sea once again rose during post-glacial times and flooded the rest of the terminal moraine between them.

The ice front remained stationary along this moraine line for some time, gradually piling up the hills of glacial boulders and gravel. The melting rate increased, however, and the ice sheet stagnated along a band several miles wide. At the same time, farther north, the still active ice began forming a second moraine. Stretching from Chatham to Woods Hole, the low hills of this

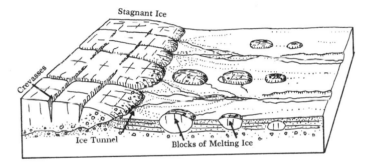

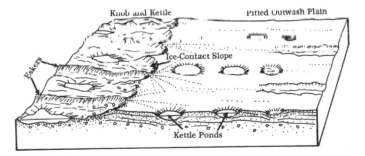

Two block diagrams showing the development of the landscape along the edge of a stagnant ice sheet (after Strahler).

second moraine form Cape Cod's upper arm bone. It reappears along the Rhode Island coast and again at Orient Point to form the northern tail of Long Island.

Outwash from the glacier at this second stopping point poured across the remnants of the ice sheet to the south burying large chunks under gravel. These pieces of ice later melted leaving irregular depressions in the outwash plain called *kettleholes*. On parts of Cape Cod the water table is near the surface and many of these kettleholes have become ponds.

Route 6, the Mid-Cape Highway, follows the crest of the Sandwich Moraine (named for one of the Cape Cod towns in which it lies) all the way from Sagamore to Dennis before dropping down onto the outwash plain. From several vantage points along the highway it is possible to look south across the flat pond-studded plain all the way to Nantucket Sound. When standing on the moraine and looking southward across the wooded Cape Cod landscape, a traveler finds it hard to believe that only yesterday in the long history of the earth, the spot where he stands marked the end of an unbroken sheet of ice stretching northward for 2,000 miles.

Places to Visit:

Nantucket Moraine, Nantucket Island and Martha's Vineyard. New England's portion of the terminal moraine of the ice sheets. See description in text. South of the moraine are gently sloping outwash plains deposited by meltwater from the ice sheet.

Sandwich Moraine and Buzzards Bay Moraine, Cape Cod. A continuous range of gravel hills that form the backbone of Cape Cod and Elizabeth Islands. Route 6, the Mid-Cape Highway, follows the Sandwich Moraine for most of its length. South of moraine is the Mashpee

Outwash Plain, a sandy plain studded with ponds and kettleholes.

Watch Hill Moraine, Rhode Island. Continuation of the Buzzards Bay Moraine along the southern coast of Rhode Island.

Books to Read:

A Geologist's View of Cape Cod by Arthur N. Strahler (Natural History Press, 1966). Excellent discussion of the evolution of Cape Cod. Covers all aspects of its geology. Compact and clearly written, useful for both amateur and serious students of Cape Cod geology.

These Fragile Outposts by Barbara Blau Chamberlain (Natural History Press, 1964). Authoritative and delightfully written, this book covers the geology, natural history, and economic development of Cape Cod and the Islands. (Out of Print)

Things Maps Don't Tell Us by A. K. Lobeck (Macmillan, 1956). Non-technical discussion of the relationship of landscape to geology. Section on Cape Cod.

The Ice Tide Ebbs

Between 15 and 20 thousand years ago, half the North American continent lay buried beneath glacial ice. Today only Greenland is still covered by a continuous ice sheet. The simplest explanation for the disappearance of the ice sheet from most of North America is one of climate change; the ice melted because the climate became warmer and perhaps drier. But what caused the changes in the climate — that precipitated the glacial epoch as well as ended it — remains one of the great unsolved geologic mysteries of the day. Nearly a dozen different theories have been proposed, but none can adequately explain all of the factual evidence.

How the ice sheet retreated, as well as how it was first formed, has also been the subject of a lively debate. Most geologists now believe that, in southern New England at least, the ice sheet stagnated and melted along bands several miles wide while the still active ice sheet piled up a new series of moraines farther north. This *stagnation zone* retreat is clearly illustrated by the two moraines in southern New England: the Nantucket Moraine and the moraines on Cape Cod. Recent investigations have disclosed two discontinuous moraines stretching from Plymouth, Massachusetts, to southern Connecticut. Between these may have been stagnant bands of ice similar to that which earlier lay between Nantucket and Cape Cod.

In several places of central and northern New England the melting of the ice sheet was interrupted by glacial readvances. The evidence for these readvances is deposits of till lying on top of meltwater gravel, indicating that the ice rode back over areas from which it had already melted. In the section on lakes we shall see

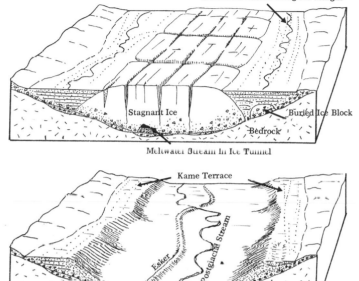

Two block diagrams showing the development of kame terraces and eskers. The ice sheet probably melted away from the higher ground first, leaving large blocks of stagnant ice in the valleys. Meltwater streams flowing along the sides of the ice masses formed kame terraces; streams flowing in tunnels beneath the ice left winding deposits of gravel known as eskers.

how one of these readvances near Middletown, Connecticut, greatly altered the subsequent geological history of the Connecticut Valley.

Glacial till, perhaps deposited by the same readvance that occurred at Middletown, forms a moraine at Cambridge, Massachusetts. This moraine appears as a low ridge running just to the west of Radcliffe College. Perhaps as geological exploration progresses, it will be possible to find other segments of this moraine between Cambridge and Middletown. Evidence for other glacial readvances occurs in Kennebunk, Maine, and St. Johnsbury and Shelburne, Vermont. Some of these may have been only local oscillations of the ice sheet; others, particularly those in northern Vermont, may have represented widespread readvances.

There is good evidence that, when the ice in an area finally stagnated, it melted on the hillsides before it melted in the valleys, and that these valley ice masses melted along their edges first. Many New England valleys are left with step-like deposits along their sides marking the sites of meltwater stream courses and temporary ponds. When the stagnant ice mass finally melted away completely, the valley-side deposits of sediments, called *kame terraces,* remained.

Some New England valleys show a series of kame terraces that look like a giant flight of steps, each level marking a place where the meltwater streams along the sides of the valleys had readjusted their courses to the dwindling ice masses in the center. The sides of the Connecticut Valley show kame terraces on a scale probably unmatched by any other New England valley. Some of these show gravelly layers deposited by running water; others are made up of finer material deposited in the still, temporary lakes along the waters of the ice margin.

The lower Connecticut Valley towns of Chester and Hadlyme exhibit a well-defined series of step-like kame terraces. Many of the tributary streams of the upper Connecticut River also exhibit impressive kame terraces along their steep valley sides. Particularly striking are those along the White River and the Ottauquechee River near White River Junction, Vermont.

In many areas these kame terraces have provided gravel for road building. Since kame terraces were formed by running water, one would expect to find more or less horizontal layers of gravel exposed in these gravel pits, but instead the gravel lies in a tumbled hodgepodge. The meltwater streams did deposit the gravel in horizontal layers but these deposits often lay against the ice masses or even on top of it. When the ice finally melted, the gravel that lay against it slumped down to produce the characteristic jumbled ice-contact slopes.

The meltwater deposits fairly well define the size and shape of the ice masses left in the valleys. Here and there it is possible to find narrow ridges of gravel pointing to the valley from the kame terraces. These mark the sites of crevasses in the ice mass which later became filled with gravel. Likewise, kettleholes in the kame terraces mark the sites of ice blocks that became separated from the main mass and were buried in the gravel. In other places the gravel-laden meltwater flowed out across the ice and filled depressions on the surface. When the ice melted these gravel-filled depressions sank to the valley floor where they now appear as irregular mounds.

Places to Visit:

Kame terraces along the Connecticut Valley and its tributary streams in New Hampshire and Vermont (see description in text). Kame terraces are very common glacial features in central and northern New England and may be seen along most of the stream valleys.

Kettleholes are extremely common on the outwash plains of Cape Cod and elsewhere. Most of the numerous ponds on Cape Cod are water-filled kettleholes.

Walden Pond, Concord, Mass. (USGS Concord). A kettle pond made famous by Henry David Thoreau. Numerous other kettleholes, some containing ponds, occur nearby.

A Book to Read:

The Surficial Geology and Pleistocene History of Vermont (Department of Water Resources, Montpelier, Vt., 1969). Data collected during an eleven year mapping program of Vermont's surficial geology. Somewhat technical. Accompanies *The Surficial Geologic Map of Vermont* (publication and map available from Vermont State Library).

Aerial photograph of an esker, Ossipee, New Hampshire. The winding gravel ridge was produced by a meltwater stream flowing in a tunnel beneath the ice. The road at the left, a two-laned cement highway, gives scale.

Eskers

Like so many abandoned railroad embankments, a number of curious gravel ridges wind across the eastern New England countryside. Known to geologists as *eskers* and to rural New Englanders — depending on locality — as whalebacks or horsebacks, these winding ridges antedate the coming of the railroads by several thousand years.

They, like most of New England's other surface features, also owe their origin to the ice sheet.

Eskers range in height up to 100 feet or more; occasionally they run unbroken for scores of miles. These gravel ridges often became paths for the Indians and early settlers; many provided a dry, open route through the heavily forested, swampy terrain that frequently lay on either side. When civilization moved in, many of the esker trails became country roads; today many eskers still have roads along their crests.

There have been several theories put forth to explain the formation of these winding gravel ridges. Most geologists believe that eskers were formed by meltwater streams flowing within the stagnant ice masses, either in crevasses or, more often, in tunnels. Like the meltwater streams flowing along the sides of the valley ice masses and forming the kames, those streams that flowed within the ice also carried along gravel and cobbles; these they deposited within the confines of their icebound channels. The streams remained on their elevated gravel beds only as long as the ice remained on either side; when it melted, the streams dropped down to the valley floors, leaving behind the winding eskers to mark their former courses.

Esker gravel is typically coarse and only crudely stratified, if at all. Confined to their narrow channels, the subglacial streams were often raging torrents capable of moving fairly large rocks. The fast-running water kept the gravel streambeds stirred up, preventing the layered formation usually associated with stream-borne deposits. However, some of the smaller eskers, usually those that probably were formed in crevasses, do show a layered sequence.

Although eskers can reach 100 feet or more in height, most tend toward the smaller end of the scale, representing accumulations from relatively small, local meltwater streams. The large eskers, on the other hand, were the beds of much larger streams. Some of these can be traced for many tens of miles, sometimes rising over hills up to 100 feet high. From this evidence geologists have inferred that not only were some of the meltwater streams quite large, but also that they were flowing in closed tunnels with enough pressure behind them to push them up and over the obstructing hills.

Eskers are fairly common in eastern and central New England. They are rare in Connecticut and Rhode Island, probably because the ice sheet in southern New England was relatively thin to begin with and broke up rapidly when it stagnated. For some as yet unexplained reason, eskers are also rare in Vermont.

Some of the longest eskers in North America are found in eastern Maine. One of these begins north of Mt. Katahdin and runs southward for 120 miles to the town of Columbia near the coast. Here the esker abruptly changes into an outwash plain about 20 miles long and 10 miles wide. The upper end of this outwash plain marked the limits of the retreating ice sheet at that time. The plain was formed when the meltwater stream burst from the confines of its tunnel and spread out across the newly uncovered land. The stream meandered, first flowing in one direction, then another, depositing layer after layer of sand and gravel. Other New England eskers end in outwash plains but none on such a grand scale as the one at Columbia. In eastern Maine there are at least a half dozen other eskers over 50 miles long. All of these long eskers have been broken into segments, however, by post-glacial streams cutting through them.

There are also several impressive eskers in New Hampshire. Route 16 parallels two of the largest: one near the Pine River in Ossipee and the other farther south in Farmington. The Farmington esker ends in an outwash plain just north of Rochester. There is another

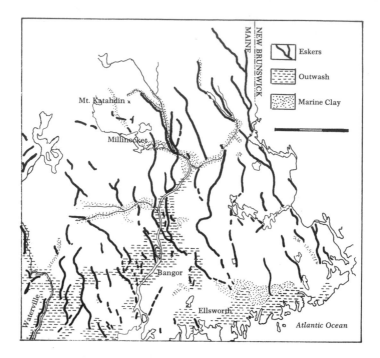

Map of eastern Maine showing eskers and other glacial features (after Atwood).

large esker that runs in segments from Lyme to West Lebanon in the Connecticut Valley. Another segmented esker runs for 20 miles along the Soucook River, a tributary of the Merrimack.

Because their gravel makes excellent road-building material, eskers near cities are becoming scarce. In eastern Massachusetts, for example, practically all of the eskers have been at least partially dug away; many have disappeared entirely. As a consequence, some effort is now being made to preserve at least portions of some of those remaining. One such esker — possibly the largest in the state — lies just to the west of Route 495 in the town of Boxborough. Already two large sections of this esker have been removed, but much of what remains is now in the hands of a conservation trust.

Places to Visit:

Enfield "Horseback," Enfield, Maine (USGS Passadumkeag). One of the many large eskers in central Maine. Route 155 runs for several miles along its top.

Eskers along Route 16, New Hampshire. Two large eskers follow east side of Route 16 for several miles at North Rochester (USGS Berwick and Alton) and at Pine River 2 miles southeast of Ossipee (USGS Wolfeboro)

Boxborough Esker, Boxborough, Mass. (USGS Ayer). Largest esker in eastern Massachusetts runs parallel to west side of Interstate 495 between Route 2 and Route 111 interchanges. Clearly seen about one mile north of Route 111 where gravel was removed for roadbuilding. Portions of esker owned by Nature Conservancy.

Other eskers may be seen in *Mohawk Mountain State Park* (see Mohawk Forest, p. 177) and in the *Pachaug State Forest* (see p. 206) in Connecticut.

The Lakes

"A mirror broken into a thousand fragments and wildly scattered over the grass," was how a contemporary of Thoreau described Maine's lake-studded countryside as he viewed it from Mt. Katahdin. The description would fit the view from many of New England's mountains, for natural lakes and ponds are very much a part of the New England scene. Practically all of these lakes and ponds are the result of glaciation. Some lie in hollows scooped out by the moving ice; others filled valleys behind dams of glacial debris; still others took shape in flooded kettleholes.

In New England, only the Green Mountains have been cheated of their share of lakes and ponds, probably because the ice sheet flowed southward along the grain of the long folds rather than across them. Elsewhere, natural lakes occur in all parts of New England.

Although there are still thousands of lakes and ponds in New England, probably many more have already vanished, particularly in the southern part. All ponds and lakes are relatively short-lived; many of those associated with the retreating glacier were especially so. Meltwater streams probably filled many with gravel; others drained when their outlet streams cut through the flimsy gravel or ice dams that were holding them.

The sites of the larger extinct glacial lakes are usually easy to spot. If the lakes lasted for any time, the accumulation of fine sediments gradually smoothed out the irregularities on the lake bottoms, producing a very flat area. The lake sediments themselves are distinctive as well. In contrast to the coarse sand and gravel deposited by streams, these lake sediments are unusually fine — mostly silt and clay. Some of the extinct glacial lake bottoms are still marshy, never having completely drained. In others, the flat ground and rich, rock-free soil make good farmland.

Some of these extinct lakes show a complex history. Many have existed at several different levels, becoming progressively lower as first one spillway and then another became ice free. These levels are often marked by elevated beaches and terraces that sometimes run for several miles along the valley sides.

Meltwater streams flowing into these glacial lakes formed deltas along their shores. These glacial lake deltas often superficially resemble kame terraces; both are

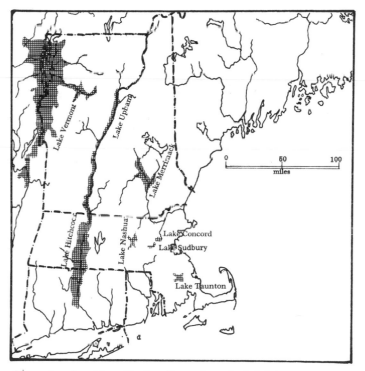

Map showing New England's major glacial lakes.

*Gravel pit in glacial lake delta, Charlestown,
New Hampshire. This delta was formed
when gravel-laden meltwater streams
hit the quiet waters of now-extinct Lake
Hitchcock. Note the diagonal layering. A
trench shovel gives scale.*

usually steep sided and often nearly flat on top. Where a gravel pit has been dug into the side of a delta, however, the difference is usually easy to see. The gravel layers in deltas are usually diagonal while these same layers in kame terraces are often jumbled where they collapsed as the ice melted from beside them.

Lake Hitchcock, the long lake that flooded the Connecticut Valley, is probably the best-known of New England's extinct glacial lakes. Lake Hitchcock began filling up when glacial debris from the Middletown readvance filled the Connecticut Valley at Rocky Hill, about 7 miles north of Middletown. As the ice sheet melted northward, the lake increased in size until it ultimately stretched about 160 miles to Lyme, New Hampshire. A second lake, that formed somewhat later, filled the northern part of the valley to the vicinity of St. Johnsbury, Vermont.

Excavations into the floor of Lake Hitchcock and several other extinct glacial lakes have revealed that some of the lake sediments occur in *varves*, a deposit of alternating layers of light-colored silt and dark-colored clay that give the deposit a banded appearance. Geologists originally believed that each varve-pair, like tree rings, represented one year's growth. The coarse silt, they believed, accumulated during the summer when more meltwater was pouring into the lake; the finer clay filtered down more slowly in the winter under the ice. By studying excavations in the lake floor at various parts of the valley geologists have counted 4,000 overlapping pairs of varves and inferred that Lake Hitchcock lasted for an equal number of years. More modern radioactive dating techniques have indicated that the lake probably lasted a far shorter time, about 2,400 years. It came to an end about 10,000 years ago when its outlet stream cut through the dam at Rocky Hill. The discrepancy between varve counts and radioactive dating remains unexplained.

After Lake Hitchcock drained, strong northwest winds blew across its bare floor, piling a series of sand dunes along the eastern side of the valley. Dunes 50 feet high and nearly 2 miles long occur at Amherst, Chicopee, and Longmeadow in Massachusetts. Smaller ones have been found in several Connecticut Valley towns to the south. When the lake floor became covered with vegetation the dune-building ceased.

The Champlain Lowland was the site of another large glacial lake, Lake Vermont. Shore terraces and beach lines of this extinct lake occur over 700 feet above the present level of Lake Champlain. As the ice retreated northward, Lake Vermont extended all the way into the St. Lawrence Valley. For a time the waters of this great lake spilled southward into the Hudson River Valley. It finally disappeared when the St. Lawrence Valley became clear of ice.

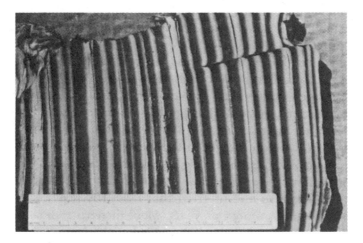

Close-up of varved clay. The light-colored bands are fine silt, probably deposited in summer. The darker clay layer may have formed beneath the ice during the winter.

There were a number of other fairly extensive glacial lakes in New England. Keene, New Hampshire, is situated on a flat lake bed. Another glacial lake filled the Merrimack River Valley in the vicinity of Concord, New Hampshire. In Massachusetts several of the major river valleys were the sites of glacial lakes. A large lake inundated most of what is now the town of Concord, and just to the south an even larger lake flooded the Sudbury River Valley for some 8 miles to Framingham. In central Massachusetts the Nashua River Valley was also filled by a large glacial lake that spilled southward through the Worcester area and later drained when the north-running Nashua Valley finally became clear of ice.

Small deltas exposed here and there in gravel pits mark the sites of many other temporary lakes that appeared in the debris-clogged valleys during the last stages of the glacial period. As investigations continue, perhaps the sites of other large glacial lakes will be found.

Places to Visit:

Glacial Lakes Hitchcock and Upham. Lake beds extend from Rocky Hill, Conn., all the way to St. Johnsbury, Vt. Varved lake sediments can be seen at many places along the riverbanks and in excavations in the valley floor. Good exposures may be seen in a large gravel pit just south of Sunderland, Mass. (USGS Mt. Toby), and high banking on east side of Route 10 about 2 miles north of Hanover, N.H.

Varved clays may also be seen in the Concord (USGS Penacook) and Keene (USGS Keene) areas of N.H. and in the Burlington (USGS Burlington) area of Vermont. Also, excellent exposures along the shores of Waterbury Reservoir (USGS Montpelier).

The Changing Sea Level

In 1848 workmen building the railroad through Charlotte, Vermont — over 150 miles from the nearest ocean — uncovered a whale skeleton. Fossils of marine animals are often found many miles from the nearest ocean, but these are almost always of some long-extinct species. The whale bones, on the other hand, must have been quite recently buried on that Vermont hillside; they belonged to a species of whale that still lives in today's oceans, and they were found in soft clay rather than petrified in solid rock.

The clay layer in which they were found blankets much of the Champlain Valley as well as a large part of eastern Maine. In both regions marine shells — many also identical to those of living organisms — are a common occurrence. These fossils — the whale skeleton and the marine shells — are conclusive evidence that both the Champlain Valley and coastal sections of Maine and New Hampshire were under the sea during fairly recent times.

The relationship of land to sea during the glacial epoch was a complicated one. When the ice sheets reached their maximum size, they buried about one-quarter of the world's land area. These great sheets of ice, probably 2 miles thick over much of their extent, locked up an immense amount of the world's water, perhaps 8 million cubic miles. As a consequence the level of the earth's great water reservoirs, the oceans, dropped about 300 feet.

Not only did the ice sheets cause the sea level to drop, their great weight also caused the land over which they moved to subside as well. Soundings in the Greenland Ice Cap show the underlying land to be over 1,000 feet

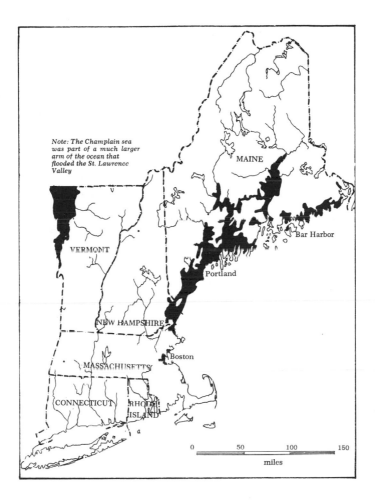

Map showing the extent of marine flooding during late-
glacial times (after Glacial Map of Eastern North America,
Geological Society of America).

below sea level. The thicker ice cap in Antarctica has depressed the underlying crust ever farther. There is plenty of evidence that the ice sheets covering North America caused a similar crustal subsidence.

As the ice sheets melted, the level of the sea once again rose. The depressed land, though relieved of its icy burden, sprang back more slowly; it also rose, but at a slower rate than did the ocean. As a result the rising ocean flooded coastal areas, depositing the layer of clay. The land, however, continued to spring back and the coastline eventually retreated to its present position.

From the geographic distribution of these clay deposits and their present height above sea level, geologists have been able to make rough estimates of how far the land subsided beneath the weight of the ice. The clay reaches its southern limit in the Boston area. South of Boston there is no evidence of coastal flooding, either because the ice sheet near its margins was not thick enough to depress the land or because not enough ice had melted during these early stages of glacial retreat to raise the sea level. Probably it was a combination of both factors.

In the Boston area, the highest exposure of marine clay is only 45 feet above the present level of the sea; most of the clay deposits are much lower. At several places around Boston the clay was dug for brick making; there are a number of abandoned clay pits in the low-lying area between Cambridge and suburban Belmont.

In coastal Maine and New Hampshire the clay covers a much wider area, forming an irregular band about 20 miles wide. It extends up some major river valleys as far as 75 miles from the present shoreline, suggesting that these river valleys were long tidal estuaries during late glacial times. In Maine some of the highest clay deposits are now 500 feet above sea level. In southern Maine the clay covers almost all of the low ground; it is exposed in

*Marine clay, Portland, Maine. A layer of
grayish clay (just above the trench
shovel) containing marine fossils resting on
light-colored glacial outwash is evidence
of an invasion of the sea shortly after the
ice melted.*

streambanks, roadcuts, and other excavations. When freshly dug the clay is gray or bluish-gray; weathering turns it to light brown.

As one might expect, the clay stretches out to sea; samples have been dredged from the shallow floor of the Gulf of Maine. How far out to sea the clay extends, like the eastern limits of the ice sheets themselves, is still unknown.

This difference in the elevations of the clay deposits, increasing from a few tens of feet above sea level near Boston to several hundred feet in Maine, is an indication that the crust was depressed to a greater depth farther north. Other evidence, such as the gentle northward tilt of the glacial lake sediments, seems to confirm this. The picture that emerges, then, is one of the ice sheet pushing down New England (and the rest of glaciated North America) into a saucer-like basin, shallow along its margins and becoming deeper toward its center.

In addition to coastal New England, the rising sea also flooded a large part of the Champlain Lowland. Glacial Lake Vermont had drained when the St. Lawrence Valley became ice-free; and shortly afterwards, salt water flooded the lake bed, leaving beach lines, fossilized shells — and a dead whale — as records of its invasion. The Champlain Sea, as this ocean arm has come to be called, covered approximately the same area as some of the lower stages of Lake Vermont. The beach lines from the sea have obscured some of the shore features produced by the earlier lake, making the exact history of this region hard to decipher. These beach and shore terraces of the Champlain Sea also tilt gently northward.

The episode of marine invasion came to an end as the land slowly sprang back. The New England coastline receded to approximately its present position; the Champlain Sea drained away, leaving the smaller present-day Lake Champlain in its place.

Although the land in many glaciated regions of the world is still rising, in coastal New England the process seems to have reversed itself. Along the coast from Massachusetts northward it is possible to find the recent remains of hardwood forests under a number of the tidal marshes. The tree stumps, still clinging to the ground in which they grew, lie preserved under layers of salt marsh peat several feet beneath the present level of the marsh. The salt marshes are an excellent measure of sea level since the most common species of grass that grows there will flourish only in the area between the tides.

Along the North River, a tidal estuary in Norwell, Massachusetts, there is a dramatic example of a recently drowned forest. Brackish water has invaded several acres of woodland; many dead tree trunks still stand in the marsh. These drowned forests are clearly seen from the bridge where Route 3 crosses the river. Along the south side of the valley, about a quarter-mile west of the bridge, the marsh has partially drowned a cedar bog, killing about half of the trees.

Other evidence for a lower sea level is the famous Boylston Street Fishweirs, a prehistoric Indian fishing site uncovered in Boston's Back Bay during building construction. These fishweirs were rows of stakes driven into what was then the bottom of a shallow bay of the Charles River. The stakes uncovered had been buried under layers of muck and peat about 12 feet below the present sea level. Most geologists believe, however, that this recent, relatively small rise in sea level represents merely a local fluctuation caused by a drop in the level of the land, rather than any definite increase in the ocean's volume.

Places to Visit:

Drowned forest at Odiorne's Point, Rye, N.H. (USGS Rye). Stumps of pine, birch, and hemlock still rooted to the soil about 2 feet below low tide.

North River, Norwell, Mass. (USGS Cohasset). Drowned forest visible from Route 3 bridge. See description in text.

It is possible to see tree stumps in several salt marshes in the Boston area. These are visible in tidal estuaries at low tide.

Books to Read:

Late Pleistocene Changes in Sea Level in Southwestern Maine by Arthur L. Bloom (Maine Dept. of Economic Development, 1960). A detailed account of late glacial history of southwestern Maine. List of fossil localities in clay. Price $1.00.

The Geology of Sebago Lake State Park by Arthur L. Bloom (Maine Dept. of Economic Development, 1959). Geological account in layman's terms of this southwestern Maine state park located within the clay belt.

The Cathedral Pines, Cornwall, Connecticut. This is probably the most magnificent stand of trees in New England. Although over 200 years old, these pines probably represent second-growth timber, perhaps springing up in an early settler's clearing.

Part II
The Vegetation

Consider how New England would look if its green mantle of vegetation suddenly disappeared. Stripped of trees and plants, the region would be nearly as stark and barren as the surface of the moon. Vegetation, therefore, is an integral part of the landscape and contributes as much in its own way to the totality of the scenery as does either the bedrock foundation or the mantle of glacial debris that we have already discussed. Furthermore, this covering of plant life is almost all-encompassing; nearly every square foot of the natural surface of the land will provide a foothold for vegetation of some kind — even boulders and rocky ledges can support a crusty growth of lichens. It is only where the land is kept in a constant state of disturbance, as on a beach, or where it is buried beneath a layer of concrete and macadam, that plants cannot grow.

New England's landscape could be described more specifically as a "treescape." Woodland now covers about three-fourths of the region; without human intervention, it would cover virtually all of it. Salt marshes and the windy summits of the highest mountains are the only natural areas that cannot support trees. As agriculture continues to decline, the woodland area continues to grow. Even the many square miles that are cleared each year to accommodate New England's expanding urban populations do not offset the gradually increasing woodland area.

As anyone who has traveled around New England will know, there are striking differences in the character of the forests from one part of the region to another. Some of these are due to climatic differences: northern Maine is almost 500 miles nearer the north pole than southern Connecticut. Some differences are due to local variations in the habitat, as for example the amount of light or moisture available to plants. Other differences in the forest from place to place reflect the enormous influence of man during his long tenure on the land. In the sections that follow we shall look at each of these forest regions, at some of the trees and plants that grow in each, and at the parts that climate, habitat, and men have played in their development.

The Geography of the Forests

In the nineteenth century, naturalists were warning New Englanders that fearful consequences would ensue if the countryside became disrobed of trees. Today, almost 100 years later, with woodland stretching from one end of the region to another, we are hard put even to understand this quaint admonition, much less to take it seriously. In the middle of the nineteenth century, however, a completely deforested southern New England, at least, did seem a real possibility. At this time somewhere between 75 and 85 percent of the region's southern half was already field and pasture. What woodlands remained were cut time and again for firewood.

Most of the present-day southern New England forests have grown within the span of human memory. Many older residents of rural areas can describe landscapes far different from the familiar wooded scene today. Old photographs showing wide expanses of open land add substance to their stories.

Most of the northern New England forests, though never cleared for farmland, are also immature. Almost every acre has been logged at least once and usually two or three times; in addition, forest fires have consumed large tracts of these northern woodlands.

Young woodlands often bear little resemblance to the mature forests that once stood in their stead. Usually an entirely different community of trees will appear in woodlands that have been logged, cleared, or burned; often centuries will pass before the forest will once more return to its original state. As the forest slowly matures, the composition of its tree community gradually changes; the sun-loving trees that first invaded the open land gradually give way to more shade-tolerant species.

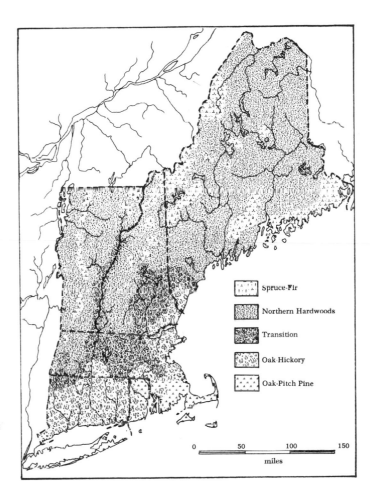

Map showing New England's forest regions (after Kuchler).

143

Much later, the forest reaches a more or less stable, self-perpetuating condition where barring further disturbance, each succeeding generation of trees is essentially of the same species as the one preceding. All over New England the forests are now in some stage of recovery, their tree communities usually representing one or another of these successional steps.

Even if New England's woodlands had not suffered extensive disturbance by man, the distribution of the forest trees might at first seem unfathomable. Some tree species have a geographic range that encompasses all of New England, but no species can grow in all of the many permutations of moisture, soil quality, and light that, taken together, describe a particular habitat. Within every square mile, often within each acre, there are noticeably different habitats, each with a correspondingly different community of trees.

In central Massachusetts, for example, it is often possible to see marked changes in the tree community merely by crossing the brow of a hill. The sunny, south-facing slope is usually clothed in oak and hickory, both characteristic of dry woodlands. Across the hill, hemlocks and maples may join the oaks to give woods on the shady, north-facing slope an entirely different flavor. Similar changes can be observed all across the forest.

In addition to the differences in the tree community resulting from local changes in the habitat, there are broad regional differences caused by a climate that becomes gradually cooler to the north. All other things being equal, the same sunny hillside that grows oaks and hickories in Massachusetts would grow spruce and balsam fir in northwestern Maine.

These three factors — man's disturbance, local habitat differences, and regional climatic differences — help to explain the seemingly chaotic distribution of tree species in the New England forests. It is the last of these, the regional differences in the forest due to climate, that provides the basis for our discussion of the forests. Often these are the hardest to see; both man's disturbance and the habitat differences obscure them to some degree.

In addition, the boundary lines between these forest types are indistinct. Because each tree species has somewhat different climatic requirements the limits of ranges do not usually coincide. As one travels from Connecticut or Massachusetts, for example, into northern New England with its cooler climate, one by one most of the trees common in the southern New England woodlands gradually become more scarce and then disappear entirely. In their stead grow more northerly species.

One of the best ways to learn about the geography of the forest is by driving the interstate highways. Avoiding populous areas as they usually do, these highways pass through forest areas far less disturbed than those along older roads. To many, the woodland scenery soon becomes monotonous, but to the few who notice the subtle changes in the character of the woodlands they pass, any long drive can be instructive.

Books to Read:

The Natural Geography of Plants by Henry A. Gleason and Arthur Cronquist (Columbia University Press, New York, 1964). An excellent introduction to plant geography for amateur naturalists. Outstanding illustrations.

The Deciduous Forests of Eastern North America by E. Lucy Braun (Hafner Publishing Co., New York, 1964). Comprehensive summary of research of this large forest area. Understandable for laymen.

Forest Ecology by Stephan Spurr (Ronald Press, New York, 1964). Study of the forest environment. Emphasis on forest management.

Silvics of Forest Trees of the United States, Agriculture Handbook 271, by H. A. Fowells (U.S. Dept. of Agriculture, 1965). Compilation of research in forest ecology, detailed range maps, life histories of forest trees. Comprehensive data on 125 tree species. (Available from U.S. Government Printing Office.)

Atlas of Forest Trees, Forest Service Miscellaneous Publication 1146 (U.S. Dept. of Agriculture 1971). Detailed range maps of all major species found in the contiguous states. Transparent overlays provide geographic data (available from U.S. Government Printing Office).

Trees: Yearbook of Agriculture, 1949 (U.S. Department of Agriculture). Covers all aspects of the forests. (Available from U.S. Government Printing Office.)

The Changing Face of New England by Betty Flanders Thomson (Macmillan, 1958). Excellent discussion of New England's vegetation. Delightfully written. (Out of Print)

New England, a Sierra Club Naturalist's Guide by Neil Jorgensen (Sierra Club 1977). First volume of a comprehensive 2 volume guide to patterns in the natural landscape that may be perceived by foot travelers. Emphasis on woodland ecology.

The Spruce-Fir Forest

Many people think of the north woods as a brooding evergreen wilderness broken only by lakes, swamps, and barren hills — a correct view perhaps of northern Canada but not of northern New England. Even some of the first people who systematically studied the New England forests shared the misconception that most of Maine and a good part of both New Hampshire and Vermont were mantled in spruce and fir. More extensive studies have shown that, although spruce and fir are both common forest trees in northern New England, the areas in which they form a solid "evergreen wilderness" are relatively small — less than one-fifth of the total area of the three northern states.

As land emerges from beneath a melting glacier, the first trees that will grow there are the spruce and balsam fir, together with a smattering of birch and poplar. In Canada this type of forest covers hundreds of thousands of square miles. The places to look for a similar type of forest in New England, then, would be in its coolest, wettest parts. And this is precisely where it is found: in northwestern Maine, northernmost New Hampshire, on the higher mountain slopes, in cold boglands, and along the cool, often foggy Maine coast.

The half-grown spruce forest — the size typical of most of New England's stands —has been aptly described as a biological desert. Few plants can survive in the deep shade cast by the closely spaced trees; often the forest floor is completely barren of vegetation. In addition, the fallen needles from the spruce trees decay slowly, producing a strongly acidic soil that is inhospitable for most plants. As the forest matures, however, competition for light and space results in a natural thinning

of the trees; eventually enough light will penetrate to encourage the growth of shrubs and young trees.

Another factor that restricts the variety of plants in the spruce-fir region is the generally harsh climate. The variety of plant life becomes progressively more attenuated in the increasingly colder climate of the north. Relatively few plants have been able to adapt to the rigorous climate that seems to favor the growth of spruce and fir.

As is true of the rest of New England's forests, few stands of spruce-fir forests have escaped the lumberman's ax. Spruce is one of the mainstays of the pulp and paper industry, and the larger trees also produce rough timber. At lower altitudes some species of spruce trees will reach from 75 to 110 feet in height. The tallest growing New England species, the red spruce, may have a trunk diameter of 3 feet, but such large trees are now rare in New England.

The other main component of the north woods, the balsam fir, our common Christmas tree, is far less valuable. This tree rarely grows taller than 60 feet and the heartwood usually starts to rot before the tree is 70 years old. Dense stands of balsam fir often appear in cutover spruce forest. In some areas the spruce trees may gradually reestablish themselves, eventually replacing the balsam fir; in others, the balsam fir remains as the dominant tree. As a result, balsam fir is becoming increasingly common in the second growth forests in northern New England. Balsam makes acceptable pulp wood but is worthless as saw timber.

As one might expect, a fire in the north woods is a disaster. Spruce and fir are relatively thin-barked

Old growth spruce-fir forest, Mt. Greylock, Massachusetts. Note the large numbers of young spruce trees growing on the forest floor.

and shallow-rooted; the resinous sap in the trunk and needles is inflammable. During particularly dry summers, the peaty forest humus becomes highly combustible; a forest fire under these conditions not only destroys the trees but burns deep into the ground, consuming the organic layer as well. And, since conifers lack the ability of some hardwoods to sprout from burned-over stumps, the return of spruce to a forest fire burn takes many years.

There are several areas of spruce-fir forest that have experienced serious fire within historical times. One of the most recent and costliest major fires occurred in the Bar Harbor region of Maine. In 1947 a dump fire that had been smoldering for a week suddenly spread to the nearby woods. The year 1947 had been one of the driest in recent history; by late summer the forests were in an explosive condition. The wind, which usually dies down after sunset, blew at gale force all night and the fire raced unchecked through the forests. For a time it looked as though the whole town of Bar Harbor was doomed; the Coast Guard prepared to evacuate the townspeople by sea. The wind shifted and, miraculously, most of the town escaped destruction. But the fire continued to burn. Before it was finally contained, over 31 square miles — most of the eastern end of the island — was a smoking ruin. The holocaust consumed 400 houses and 17,000 acres of mature spruce and white pine forest.

Today, almost a quarter of a century later, the destruction caused by the fire is still painfully apparent. In place of the spruce and pine, the hills around Bar Harbor are now clothed with a scraggly thicket of birch, wild cherry, poplar, and sumac, the usual trees to repopulate a burn. Worse yet, the ground was so dry in 1947 that the fire consumed almost all of the humus that had been accumulating on the forest floor, leaving behind nothing but a sterile covering of broken rock,

*Painted trillium. A common spring
wildflower found in the spruce-fir forest
region.*

which subsequent rains washed from the steeper slopes, denuding them even more. It will be at least a lifetime — perhaps several — before the rocky hills on Mt. Desert Island are once again covered with a mature spruce forest.

Insect attack has also wreaked a fearful toll on the New England spruce forest. Between 1909 and 1918 the spruce budworm invaded Maine and destroyed about 70 percent of all the spruce and fir trees in the state — enough wood to keep the papermills operating for about 20 years. The outbreak seems to have been encouraged by the abundance of second-growth balsam fir, a tree that is initially more susceptible to the insect. The epidemic spread rapidly; at the time there was no effective means to combat it. There have been no serious outbreaks of the budworm attack since 1917, but if there should be in the future, control would probably be possible.

Wind has been another great enemy of the spruce forests. Hurricanes such as the 1938 disaster and the less severe storms of the middle fifties toppled many of the shallow-rooted spruce and firs, particularly in stands that had already been thinned out by attacks of the budworm or by cutting. But, as we shall see in a later section, the damage to the spruce forests has been relatively minor in comparison to the devastation of the white pines caused by the 1938 hurricane.

On the slopes of some of the northern peaks in the Mt. Katahdin group, the spruce forest exhibits a curious phenomenon. Long strips of dead trees follow the mountainside like contour lines, giving them a banded appearance. The pattern resembles the ripple-like waves that one sees when a light breeze blows across a grainfield; only here the ripples are permanently impressed in the forest as lines of toppled trees. Investigators first thought the patterned bands were blowdowns from the

1938 hurricane, but older mountain men recall seeing them prior to 1938. In addition, many of the dead trees are still standing.

More recent study seems to indicate that these "blow-downs" are slowly migrating up the mountain slopes. If the bands were moving in the downslope, they might possibly be attributed to gradual movement of the mantle rock, a slowly creeping landslide. But, each year, along their upper leading edges, the mature trees die and are systematically replaced by seedlings which then grow to maturity. The upward movement of these bands defies explanation.

The soil beneath the spruce forest is nearly always infertile. Often a hole dug in the forest floor will reveal a curious layer of grayish-white sand beneath the usually thick layer of sticks and decaying spruce needles. Soils exhibiting this same grayish layer almost directly beneath the forest mold have been found in other northern regions. Russian scientists, the first group to study soils, called this type of soil a *podzol*, the Russian word meaning "ash-soil," after the resemblance of the gray layer to wood ashes.

As is true of all soils, the development of podzols is intimately related to climate, the underlying rock, and the vegetation cover. In New England podzol soils develop in a cool, moist climate where the underlying glacial till came mainly from granitic rocks. The humus layer beneath spruces and other conifers is strongly acidic; rainwater seeping through the humus becomes charged with acid. Although this acid is quite dilute, it slowly percolates through the glacial till below, dissolving away all of the minerals save the quartz. Hence, the ashy gray layer characteristic of podzols is predominantly quartz. Quartz adds no nutrients to the soil; the leached, sterile layer is of no benefit to the plant life above.

There are a few areas of virgin spruce-fir forest still left in northern New England. A magnificent 125-acre stand grows at Norton Pool, near Pittsburg in extreme northern New Hampshire. This forest is mainly balsam fir, but scattered spruces — some of which reach 90 feet in height — also grow there. The St. Regis Paper Company, owner of the land, has generously set the area aside for preservation.

Another stand of virgin forest, about 510 acres in extent, grows in "The Bowl" on Mt. Whiteface, near Waterville, New Hampshire. The elevation of this forest ranges from 1,900 feet on the floor of the Bowl up to 4,000 feet on its sides. As a consequence, the forest shows the typical zonation that one finds in the mountains — beech, maple, and birch at lower elevations; spruce and balsam higher up.

A third area of virgin forest, remote and inaccessible, lies on the upper reaches of Nancy Brook, a small stream that tumbles down into the Saco River Valley about 3 miles south of Crawford Notch, New Hampshire. The trees in this 500-acre tract are of all ages and sizes, ranging from seedlings to very large specimens.

There are other smaller patches of virgin spruce-fir forest here and there on the upper slopes of the White Mountains. These high altitude stands are almost always too stunted by the harsh climate to have been of much commercial value, hence were never logged. Although the trees at these higher altitudes are smaller, the tracts exhibit the characteristics of the virgin forests: trees of many different ages and sizes growing together, mature trees spaced widely apart, and the forest floor covered with a luxuriant carpet of mosses and other plants. The Great Gulf on Mt. Washington's north slope and the Chimney Pond Area on Mt. Katahdin both have substantial areas of high-altitude virgin forests.

Places to Visit:

Mt. Desert Island, Maine (USGS Bar Harbor and Mt. Desert). The site of a disastrous forest fire that blackened the eastern side of the Island. Mature spruce-fir forest still covers much of the unburned portions.

Virgin Spruce-Fir Forest at Norton Pool, Pittsburg, N.H. (USGS Second Lake). See description in text. Permission to visit the area and directions may be obtained from F. W. Cowan, Resident Manager, St. Regis Paper Co., West Stewartstown, N.H.

"The Bowl," Mt. Whiteface, Waterville, N.H. (USGS Mt. Chocorua). See description in text. Off Tom Wiggin Trail. Virgin forest in western end of Bowl. Part of White Mountain National Forest.

Nancy Brook Virgin Forest, Livermore Twp., N.H. (USGS Crawford Notch). See description in text. May be reached by Mt. Bemis Trail, thence up the Nancy Pond Trail or up the brook.

"Blowdowns" on Mt. Katahdin Area, Maine (USGS Katahdin). See description in text. Pattern of dead trees conspicuous on "The Owl" and several other peaks on northwest side of the range. Visible from Tableland or from Hunt Trail.

Camels Hump Fir Forest, Duxbury, Vt. (USGS Camel's Hump) Boreal Forest near the summit of Camel's Hump Mountain.

Above the Treeline:
New England's Alpine Zone

The most spectacular scenery in New England may be viewed from the barren summits of its highest mountains. The mountaintops themselves, often resembling huge rock piles, present an other-worldly appearance. The intense frost at these high altitudes has broken loose great slabs of bedrock that often rest precariously

Aerial photograph of the alpine zone of the Presidential Range, New Hampshire. A dusting of snow highlights the treeless area of New Hampshire's highest mountains. Six-thousand-foot Mt. Washington is just to the right of center.

on one another. The distant views — on a clear day — are also splendid; sometimes it is possible to see 75 miles or more across the mountains and valleys, dark green woods, and sparkling lakes.

On high mountains, however, clear days are the exception rather than the rule. Often when sun is shining in nearby valleys, the mountaintops are locked in thick clouds, and the weather there is as cold and raw as in November. On the peaks of the Presidential Range in New Hampshire's White Mountains, snow falls even in summer and the temperature at night often drops below freezing.

Summer weather on these mountaintops is often unpleasant; the winter weather, fierce beyond belief. The records of the year-round weather station atop Mt. Washington give a measure of just how bad the weather is. Over 70 inches of precipitation falls on Mt. Washington annually, mostly as snow. There are weeks at a time when the temperature does not rise above zero. But probably more than anything else it is the wind on Mt. Washington that justifies its reputation for having the worst weather in the world. Winds of hurricane force are common. In a storm on April 12, 1934, the weather station recorded a wind velocity of 231 miles per hour, about one-third the velocity of a shotgun blast.

It is no wonder that, in a climate such as this, trees cannot survive. On the mountaintops, wind is the great enemy of trees. Even despite the high precipitation, the constant wind literally blows the moisture right out of the trees. During most of the year the temperature stays below freezing and the trees cannot replenish this lost moisture from the frozen ground. Temperature is also an important limiting factor to the growth of trees. Drifts of snow will prevent new growth and seed germination; the growing season for a tree cannot begin until the snow around its branches has melted. Even boreal

Winter on Mt. Washington, New Hampshire. The treeless summit of the mountain is reputed to experience the worst winter weather in the United States. Note the chains to hold down the building on the left.

tree species such as black spruce and balsam fir need a growing season of 8 weeks with an average temperature of at least 50° F. for seeds to germinate and new wood to ripen.

Climbing a mountain is like traveling north. In moist temperate regions such as New England, each 400 feet in elevation produces the same climate found 100 miles farther north (all other things being equal). This effect can be clearly seen in the changing vegetation on New England's mountains.

Except for the trails up the west side of Mt. Washington beginning at an elevation of 2,000 feet, most of the trails up New England's higher mountains begin in the familiar northern hardwood forest. The most common trees here are sugar maple, beech, and silver birch, with a scattering of balsam and spruce. As a person climbs higher, the woods become wetter and gradually take on a more northerly aspect. The spruce and balsam increase in number. Maples and beech disappear, leaving the silver birch as the common deciduous tree. The border between the northern deciduous forest and the boreal conifer forest is fairly distinct on the mountain slopes. The spruce and balsam increase until the woods become almost solid stands of evergreens. Deciduous trees and shrubs cannot survive the dense shade of the evergreens, but grow only in spots where there is sun.

Gradually all the deciduous trees disappear, leaving pure stands of spruce and balsam. These trees become progressively shorter and more gnarled and twisted against the harsh winds. Finally the trees are not really trees at all but merely dense, prostrate mats rising only a foot or two above the ground. This gnarled, prostrate growth is known as *Krummholz,* a German word meaning "crooked wood." Most botanists believe Krummholz results from a combination of snow and wind. At these high elevations the trees can survive the winter only under the snow. Although snow prevents new growth in the summer, it makes a fine insulator in winter. The snow remains close to freezing and thus may be as much as 70° warmer than the frigid air temperature above it. The wind cannot penetrate the snowbank, and the moist snow packed around the trees further retards water loss. At these elevations the blast of the wind will kill any part of the tree which has grown above the snow, while the protected lower branches can survive under its blanket. Each year the horizontal growth continues, while the vertical growth is killed off by the wind and cold.

Unlike the other forest boundaries, the tree line is abrupt. Patches of Krummholz persist here and there in sheltered spots, but finally a point is reached on the mountain where Krummholz cannot extend one foot higher. As one might expect, this elevation is determined by several factors. Shelter from the prevailing wind and average temperature vary from one side of the mountain to another. As a result the treeline is several hundred feet higher on the sunny south-facing slopes than on the exposed northern slopes. In New Hampshire these elevations are about 5,200 feet and 4,800 feet, respectively. Latitude is another factor which affects the elevation of the treeline. On more northerly Mt. Katahdin, the treeline is about 500 feet lower than in New Hampshire.

Relatively few of New England's mountains are high enough to exhibit a treeless alpine zone. New Hampshire's Presidential Range has nearly 8 square miles above the treeline; a smaller but still impressive alpine zone covers the top of Mt. Katahdin. A number of other mountains in New Hampshire, Vermont, and Maine have no trees or only Krummholz at their summits. The summits of several of these lie below the natural treeline; the absence of trees there is the result of fire or

Above the timberline, Presidential Range, New Hampshire. Note the cover of dwarf plants.

lumbering. Natural reforestation is slow on the exposed summits of these lower mountains.

Returning to our climatic equation — each 400 feet in elevation produces roughly the same climate as that 100 miles farther north — we can calculate that the climate at the 5,000 foot timberline is about the same as that of northern Quebec. If anything, the mountaintop with its constant wind and high precipitation is even harsher.

It may seem surprising that anything will grow above the treeline, yet plant life here, as nearly everywhere, fills almost every available sheltered crevice in the rocks. Even the rocks themselves support several species of lichens. Sedges and mosses, the chief plants of the tundra, thrive in the peaty mountain soil. In addition, about 110 species of flowering plants grow in this inhospitable environment. Of these, about 35 species are more common in the spruce-fir forests at lower elevations; the other species — about 75 — are commonly found only above the treeline. Many of these same alpine plants are also found on the arctic tundra of northern Canada.

The little alpine plants on the mountaintops are wonderfully adapted for conserving moisture. Most grow no more than a few inches above the ground; many are prostrate. The plants often grow in such tight clumps that they retain last year's dead leaves and form tiny cushions which act as reservoirs for holding moisture as well. Many of their leaves are thick and leathery, often covered with hairs or wax to further conserve moisture. The low growth habit of these plants also provides them with the same advantage in the winter that we observe in the Krummholz vegetation, permitting them to spend the coldest time of the year in the moisture and relative warmth of a snowdrift.

Many of these little alpine plants produce bright flowers. The height of the flowering season is about the last week in June on the Presidential Range and a week or two later on Katahdin.

During this time the barren slopes of the alpine zone are transformed into a giant rock garden. From the rock crevices spring clumps of tiny white, yellow, and bright pink flowers. Probably the most spectacular display is on a flat area just above the headwall of Tuckerman's Ravine, aptly called "The Alpine Garden." Here clumps of flowers sometimes 10 feet square blaze against the somber greens of sedge and scattered Krummholz. Bigelow Lawn, about a mile south of the summit, also presents a fine flower display.

Although the Presidential Range and Mt. Katahdin have the most extensive collection of arctic plants, the bare summits of other New England mountains have their share as well. A number of these are listed at the end of this section.

The southernmost mountain in New England to exhibit a variety of alpine plants is Mt. Monadnock. With an elevation of only 3,000 feet, the mountain lies well below the true treeline; its upper slopes, however, are largely barren of trees. The treeless slopes and summit are thought to be the result of repeated fires intentionally set by early settlers to drive out wolves that lived there. Trees have been slow in reestablishing themselves on the exposed mountainsides, and a number of alpine plants flourish, particularly on the cooler northwestern slope.

Most of the mountains of New England are wilderness country. The best way to explore them is on foot. Most of the trails are well marked and vary in steepness. Hiking through the rugged terrain is hard work, but not nearly as hard as many people think. There is much to be seen along the mountain trails; the hiker who travels slowly and stops frequently to examine his surroundings or to enjoy the view from a break in the woods will find most climbs not too difficult. Fatigue is the greatest when a person has the single-minded goal of reaching the top in the shortest possible time.

Nevertheless, the mountains make certain demands upon a person. It is important to have all of the following before starting on a trip: comfortable hiking shoes (not sneakers), food, warm clothing, raingear, a trail map, some physical endurance, and good sense. When traveling above the treeline, one should be particularly cautious. Practically all of the regularly maintained trails are well-defined paths on the wooded mountain slopes; above the treeline, however, they often become merely a line of rock cairns or paintblazes on the rocks that may be hard to follow in bad weather. Moreover, the open country offers no shelter. Scores of people have become lost and many have died of exposure to the harsh climate above the treeline.

The alpine zone of the Presidential Range is accessible to nearly everyone. In addition to the many hiking trails that reach above the timberline, there is a toll road and a cog railway to the summit of Mt. Washington, the highest peak. Naturalists who are not up to the arduous climb on foot can reach the summit by car or by train, spend the day exploring the alpine zone, then return to the summit and ride back down. Turnouts along the toll road allow the chance to stop for a closer look at the trees and plants along the way.

Places to Visit:

Alpine Zone of Presidential Range, N.H. (USGS Mt. Washington). Extensive area above timberline. Alpine zone may be reached by road from Pinkham Notch by cog railway from west side of Mt. Washington or by foot via one of a number of trails. Hotel on summit of Mt. Washington. In the Presidential Range and other parts of White Mountains the Appalachian Mountain Club maintains 9 mountain hostels that provide food and lodging for hikers. Four of these are on Presidential Range. A brochure, *A.M.C. Hut System,* available from Appalachian Mountain Club headquarters. Third week in June is height of wildflower season in Presidential Range.

Weather Station on Mt. Washington.. Interesting little museum contains geological, meteorological, and historical information about Mt. Washington.

Alpine Zone on Mt. Katahdin (USGS Katahdin). Treeless area similar to that of Presidential Range. Accessible only by foot. Essentially the same arctic alpine flora as Presidential Range.

Mt. Monadnock, Jaffrey, N.H. (USGS Monadnock). Small area of alpine vegetation on northwest side of mountain. Excellent views. Easy climb.

Other New England mountains exhibiting alpine vegetation include: Mt. Mansfield and Camel's Hump in Vermont; the Franconia Range, Cannon Mountain, Mt. Guyot, Baldface Mountain, Mt. Moosilauke, Mt. Chocorua, Mt. Cardigan in New Hampshire; Mt. Bigelow, Old Speck Mountain, Baldpate, Mt. Abraham, Moxie Bald Mountain, Sugarloaf Mountain, and Saddleback Mountain in Maine.

Books to Read:

Mountain Flowers of New England by Evelyn Underhill (Appalachian Mountain Club, 1977). Indispensable guide to trees and flowers of the mountains. Many color photographs.

Alpine Zone of the Presidential Range by L. C. Bliss, 1963 (available from Appalachian Mountain Club, $1.25). Comprehensive discussion of geology, climate, flora, and fauna of area above the timberline. Nontechnical.

The Appalachian Trail by Ann and Myron Sutton (Lippincott, 1967). Interesting account of the 2,050-mile-long mountain trail that runs from Maine to Georgia.

The Appalachians by Maurice Brooks (Houghton Mifflin, 1965). This handsome book describes the natural history of the mountain region. Emphasis is chiefly on the Southern Appalachians, but the book contains a section on Alpine Zones of New England.

A.M.C. White Mountain Guide, 1976 (available from Appalachian Mountain Club, $8.00). Hiker's guide to all the White Mountains. Eight maps.

A.M.C. Maine Mountain Guide, 2nd ed., 1976 (available from Appalachian Mountain Club, $6.50). Complete guide to Maine mountains. Special attention given to Katahdin and Mt. Desert Regions.

Mount Washington and *Winter on Mt. Washington* (Mount Washington Observatory, 1962). Two informative booklets about New England's highest mountain. *Mount Washington* has a fold out center page that identifies the other mountains visible from Mt. Washington's summit.

Swamps and Bogs

If Robert Frost had been a geologist instead of a farmer he might have written, "Something there is that doesn't love a pond." Ponds, like New England stone walls, appear to be among the more permanent features of the landscape, but nature seems to love neither. Stone walls topple with the frost and ponds slowly fill in and disappear.

New England is still a land of natural lakes and ponds. Ten thousand years ago, when the land became ice-free, there were even more than there are today. In addition to the great glacial lakes, water stood in many of the low spots in the hummocky layer of glacial debris that covered the land. But ponds and lakes are among the most temporary of geologic phenomena. As soon as these appeared, the forces of nature began the process of eradicating them. Streams that fed the ponds carried silt into them. Aquatic plants that grew along the shallow shores contributed their organic debris to the muddy layers on the bottom. Today, 10,000 years later, many low spots that were once open water are now swamps, bogs, or low woodland.

The succession from open water to dry land follows several different routes. These depend mostly on climate and the quality of the underlying mantle rock. In southern New England, a reedy marsh is the usual step between ponds and dry land. Waterlilies and floating aquatic plants are the first clearly visible harbingers of the pond's ultimate destruction. Reeds, cattails, and bulrushes follow, growing outward from the shore and gradually spreading across the increasingly shallow pond bottom. This vegetation in turn contributes to the layer of organic debris on the bottom, eventually pro-

Spruce bog, Ashburnham, Massachusetts.
The trees and shrubs in the foreground
have formed a floating mat that is gradually
growing across the pond.

viding a footing for swamp shrubs such as buttonbush, alder, sweet gale, willow, and sweet pepperbush, all of which grow happily in the water-logged muck of the drying pond. These shrubs in turn draw more moisture out of the muck until eventually it becomes dry enough to support trees of the swamp forest: white ash, red maple, and elm. Across southern New England it is possible to find examples of pond succession at every stage.

Along the coast and on higher ground, where the climate is cool and moist, the change from pond to forest follows a different route. Along the way there may be produced one of the most interesting of botanical habitats, the quaking bog.

Like marshes, bogs begin as ponds; many active bogs still have areas of open water in the middle. A floating mat of sphagnum moss, sedge, and other plants gradually grows outward from the shores and will eventually — if the climate does not change — bridge the whole pond. In time this mat will thicken enough to support shrubs, small trees, and people. But, because it is floating on the surface of the pond, the flexible mat will quake and shudder when walked upon.

The type of plants that grow in a bog is what distinguishes it from a marsh. All of these plants have several common characteristics, one of which is that they can survive in a nutrient-free environment. For, in addition to being soggy and waterlogged, the bog habitat is usually impoverished of plant nutrients. Bogs are common in areas underlain by granitic rocks. In a previous section we saw that sandy glacial till derived from granite provides the plants with few nutrients. In most bogs there is a shortage of lime and phosphorus, both important to the growth of many plants. Consequently, the bog flora is restricted in part to species that can survive without these.

A layer of sphagnum of the thickness commonly found in the bog mat is almost as impervious to the flow of water as is a layer of rock. Sphagnum can hold many times its own weight in water but the sogginess of the bog mat is almost always caused by rain water rather than by pond water percolating into the sphagnum from below. Rain water contains even fewer plant nutrients than does the pond water, thus depriving the bog plants even more.

Another characteristic of bog plants is their ability to grow in a strongly acidic habitat. The sodden layer of sphagnum prevents air from traveling downward, thereby retarding the decay of dead layers below. The type of decay that does take place in the airless, wet environment beneath the surface produces the highly acidic conditions so characteristic of most bogs. In addition, this type of decay robs bogs of available nitrogen, another important nutrient.

The layers of dead sedge and sphagnum accumulate faster than they decay, eventually forming a solid organic deposit in the bottom of the bog. This is the source of peat moss widely used in gardening.

Predictably, the plant species that can survive in this inhospitable habitat have unusual characteristics. Although moisture is everywhere, the high acidity makes it difficult for most plants to absorb water. It is not surprising, then, that common bog shrubs — bog laurel, rhodora, labrador tea, and the aptly-named leatherleaf — have small leathery or woolly leaves to retard the loss of moisture. Other bog plants such as sundew, pitcher plants, and butterwort have solved the problem of nitrogen deficiency in a bizarre way — by trapping and di gesting insects.

The bog flora is interesting in other ways. The unusual conditions present in bogs have made them the meeting place for both arctic and tropical plants. Leather-leaf, labrador tea, and cotton grass, all common on the arctic tundra, grow side by side with insectivorous plants and bog orchids that surely had their origin in the tropics. High acidity and low nutrients are also characteristic of soils in the tropical rain forest. It is not surprising, then, that some genera of these mostly tropical

Pitcher plant. A bog plant that obtains nitrogen by capturing and digesting insects in the water-filled, pitcher-like leaves.

plants have moved into the cooler but otherwise similar habitats of the northern bogs.

As the mat grows toward the center of the pond, the shrubs that ring the outer edges of the bog follow along behind. These shrubs shade out the smaller bog plants. Trees follow the shrubs and in turn shade them out. The ultimate end of bog succession, then, is a wet forest. The sodden, acid environment approximates that of the boreal spruce forest; in northern New England black spruce along with larch and balsam are common bog trees. Along the coast, from eastern Connecticut to southern Maine, Atlantic white cedar invades bogland. The white cedar usually grows in such dense stands that it often shades out all other trees.

If a climate already conducive to bog growth becomes even more moist, bog succession may go in the opposite direction; instead of forest gradually growing out across the bog, the bog may expand outward into the forest. Sphagnum moss, because of its ability to trap rainwater, may in time grow higher than the forest floor around it and gradually grow outward among the trees, eventually drowning their roots and killing them. Some bogs in eastern Maine seem to be expanding in this manner.

America has inherited a rich, though sinister, bog mythology from Europe. On both sides of the Atlantic, many people still regard bogs as unsavory places fraught with quicksand and other dangers. The tales of pixies and heathens, the strange, mythical inhabitants of European bogland, do have some historical basis in fact. The bog dwellers were merely primitive people who were driven into the inhospitable environment of bogs and heaths by the Romans and early Christians. The Seminole Indians in Florida have received similar treatment from the white man in this country.

Later, and probably as a direct result of this earlier mythology, European bogs acquired a further evil repu-

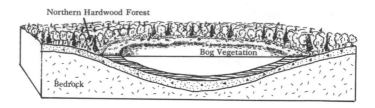

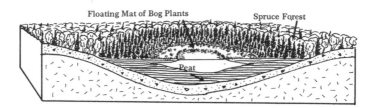

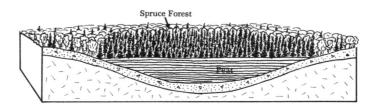

Three block diagrams showing the development of a spruce bog.

tation by being made the setting for many a horror story. Arthur Conan Doyle in *The Hound of the Baskervilles* has one of his characters describe the "Great Grimpen Mire," a particularly unwholesome stretch of British bogland, as a place where "a false step yonder means death to man or beast." Perhaps cows and horses did occasionally wander into a bog and break through the mat. The possibility of a similar fate befalling a human being is small. Stepping into a hole might mean a muddy leg, but rarely more. In case of the infinitely small probability of carelessly blundering with both feet into a hole, a person should remain calm and wait for a companion to assist him. He emphatically will not be sucked down. Holes in the floating mat do occasionally exist, but these are easily avoided by walking gingerly and avoiding wet spots, particularly those covered by a coarse, bright green species of sphagnum moss.

A false step in a New England bog, from southern New Hampshire southward, is more likely to carry a person into a clump of poison sumac than into bottomless quicksand. But neither the danger of poison sumac nor the small possibility of stepping through the mat should deter naturalists from exploring bogs. Poison sumac is easily recognized as the only bog shrub with small compound leaves and clusters of whitish berries in summer and fall.

The unusual and rare plants are the main attraction of bogs. Of these, the bog orchids probably arouse the most interest among naturalists. Although the bog orchids are among the most beautiful of wildflowers, their relatively small size often proves disappointing to the novice who expects to find flowers as large as those of tropical species. Each species of orchid has its own blooming period, usually sometime between mid-May and late June. Several visits to a bog during this time may turn up different species in flower. A number of other bog plants and shrubs have colorful spring flowers.

Occasionally, people attempt to transplant the bog orchids to their home grounds — almost always without success. It is easy to infer from their very rarity that these orchids have exacting requirements. Not one gardener in a thousand can reproduce the proper conditions to grow them successfully. In addition, digging up wild orchids is unlawful in some New England states.

There are several well known bogs in New England. The Wildflower Society owns two of them: the Bugbee Bog in Peacham, Vermont, and the Bradford Bog in Bradford, New Hampshire. The latter is an example of bog succession in its last stages; all vestiges of the pond and quaking mat have disappeared. The Nature Conservancy owns a quaking bog in Norwell, Massachusetts. As in most coastal bogs a stand of Atlantic white cedar is growing outward onto the mat. Another bog, Big Heath, in the Seawall section of Maine's Acadia National Park, is the largest of several on park property.

There are many other less well-known but equally interesting bogs in New England. In Connecticut, Rhode Island, and southeastern Massachusetts there are a number of large cedar bogs. In northern New England, spruce bogs are common, particularly at higher elevations. In northern Maine and along the valley of Vermont there are several "sweet" bogs where the underlying limestone rock has neutralized the acidity of the peat. This unusual habitat supports an equally unusual flora.

Bogs can be read from topographic maps, usually (but not always) as rounded ponds ringed by a circle of swampland. If the map has woodlands designated on it, the green overprint signifying woodland usually stops short of the pond's shoreline, indicating the open bog mat surrounding the shore. In the spruce-fir region and the cooler parts of the northern hardwood forest, almost every area shown as swampland will be bog.

Places to Visit:

Bradford Bog, Bradford, N.H. (USGS Lovewell Mtn.). Owned by New England Wildflower Society. One mile east of village, East Washington. Marked trails.

Black Pond, Norwell, Mass. (USGS Cohasset). Mt. Blue Street, .7 mile from junction with Central Street. Unmarked turnoff on right-hand side. Quaking cedar bog owned by Nature Conservancy.

Big Heath, Southwest Harbor, Maine. (USGS Swan Island). One-quarter mile west of Seawall Campground, Acadia National Park. One of several bogs on park property

Great Meadows, Concord, Mass. (USGS Concord). Route 62, 1.3 miles east of Concord Center, turn left on Monson Rd. Typical freshwater marsh habitat. Owned by the U.S. Fish and Wildlife Service.

Heath Pond Bog, Ossipee, N.H. (USGS Ossipee). Near Ossipee-Effingham line, a short distance southwest of Route 25. Classic example of bog succession. Rich bog flora.

Mud Pond Bog, Fox State Forest, Hillsboro, N.H. (USGS Hillsboro). Trails lead to the bog from Forest Headquarters. Typical bog flora.

Black Spruce Bog, Mohawk Forest, Goshen, Conn. (USGS Cornwall). Near ranger headquarters, south of Route 4. Boardwalk into bog. Description of formation and plants to be seen.

Shade Swamp Sanctuary, Farmington, Conn. (USGS New Britain). Off Route 6, one mile west of intersection with Route 10. *Field Guide* to sanctuary describing plant life published by Farmington River Watershed Association, Avon, Conn., 50¢.

Dead Creek Waterfowl Area, Addison, Vt. (USGS Port Henry, N.Y.–Vt.). The largest waterfowl management area in Vermont. Typical marsh vegetation, 1000 acres.

Books to Read:

Reading the Landscape by May Theilgaard Watts (Macmillan, 1957). Informal study of ecology. Chapters on swamps and bogs. Emphasis is chiefly on midwestern United States but much is applicable to New England landscape.

Inland Wetland Plants of Connecticut by William E. Niering and Richard H. Goodwin (Connecticut College, New London, 1973). Excellent small guide to common plants of the various freshwater wetland communities. Most species described are found across much of New England.

The Northern Hardwood Forests

In the areas where soil and climate are more hospitable, the spruce-fir forests gradually give way to a more varied assemblage of trees, usually called the "northern hardwood forest." This forest name, however, is somewhat misleading. A trio of hardwoods — birch, beech, and maple —are the dominant trees in much of northern New England, but spruce, hemlock, and white pine — all conifers — are very abundant in some areas.

As with the spruce-fir forests, the boundaries of the northern hardwoods seem closely related to climate. This mixture of conifers and hardwoods covers most of northern New England. In Maine it reaches as far south as Portland; it covers the northern two-thirds of New Hampshire and practically all of Vermont. A tongue of northern hardwoods stretches southward from Vermont across the Berkshires of western Massachusetts into northwestern Connecticut.

Where hardwoods predominate, the forests present an entirely different appearance from the typical second-growth spruce-fir forests. Instead of dark, almost stifling interiors so common in half-grown coniferous forests, the hardwood canopy is much more open, providing enough light to support a variety of shrubs and plants on the forest floor.

This is the forest region of brilliant fall color. From the middle of September in the northern mountains to the middle of October farther south, the summer green of the forest changes into an almost indescribable array of color. The maples turn bright red or orange; the birch, beech, and larch a golden yellow. Red oak and ash, also locally abundant members of the forest, both lend their splash of color to the display. Where conifers abound, their somber green background seems to high-light the colors of the hardwoods even more.

The forest soils underlying the northern hardwoods are generally better than those beneath the conifers. Hardwood trees are more likely to colonize fertile sites, and once established they actually improve the soil rather

(*Photo:* Barbara B. Paine)

Two wildflowers common in the northern
hardwood forest: Dutchman's-breeches
(above) and bluebead lily (on facing
page). Dutchman's-breeches prefers
a neutral soil while the more northerly
growing bluebead lily thrives in an acid
soil.

than impoverish it. The leaves of these trees decay rapidly on the forest floor and, except for the oaks, do not produce strong organic acids. As a result, the underlying humus stays sweet and the soil beneath it does not develop the gray podzol layer. The deep roots of the hardwoods further enrich the soil by loosening it, allowing air and organic matter to penetrate more deeply. Where conifers are abundant, however, the soils are usually podzols or will in time become so.

Fire is not nearly as great an enemy of the mature northern hardwood forest as it is of the spruce-fir forests. The thick bark and deep roots of the hardwood make them much more fire-resistant. Even the leafy forest floor is less flammable. Normally a fire in the hard-

(*Photo*: Barbara B. Paine)

wood forest will merely burn the shrub layer and plants on the forest floor. But in dry years, particularly in tracts where conifers are abundant, there have been disastrous fires in this type of forest as well.

Wind is also less damaging to hardwoods. The deep-rooted trees are usually firmly anchored to the ground. In a mixed forest the hardwoods act as windbreaks, protecting the more shallowly rooted conifers from the full force of high winds. A tree's susceptibility to wind damage or blowdown, however, increases as the tree grows older. A bad hurricane may be almost as disastrous to old stands of hardwoods as it is to conifers.

A far greater peril to the hardwood forests is attacks by insects or disease. In recent years epidemics have wreaked a dreadful toll on certain tree species in the northern hardwood forests. Man has probably been the chief cause of these serious outbreaks. His widespread disturbance of the forests by both cutting and burning has often upset the delicate ecological balance, opening the way for insect attack.

In the early part of this century, a fungus plague wiped out about a quarter of the beech trees in northern New England. Although beech is a beautiful forest tree, its wood is not particularly valuable; hence the epidemic, though serious, was not an economic disaster.

The devastation wrought by the birch borer was another story. Between 1939 and 1952 this insect destroyed about 70 percent of the white and yellow birch in northern New England. Birch is the most valuable of the northern hardwoods; this destruction amounted to a huge economic loss for forest owners. Today, from almost any high point in the northern forest, it is still possible to see the gaunt skeletons of dead birches here and there among living trees.

There is the ever-present danger that one or another of the insect or fungus plagues will return to the northern hardwood region. Since the forest is a major economic resource of northern New England, foresters and entomologists keep careful watch for signs of disease. With modern methods to combat them, most forest epidemics can be controlled if detected early enough.

Places to Visit:

Plainfield Hardwood Slope, Plainfield, N.H. (USGS Hanover). Detailed directions obtainable from the New England Wildflower Society, owners. Section of mature northern hardwoods with wide assortment of wildflowers.

Margaret Perry Woods, Hancock, N.H. (USGS Monadnock). Permission to visit area and detailed directions may be obtained from College Forester, Dartmouth College, Hanover, N.H. Northern hardwood forest growing on very rocky terrain. Undisturbed for at least 60 years.

Gifford Woods, Rutland, Vt. (See description, page 190)

Concord Sugar Maple Beech Forest, Concord, Vt. (USGS Littleton, N.H.–Vt.). Old growth deciduous tract of about 140 acres. Owned by University of Vermont. Permission to visit and directions may be obtained from Botany dept.

Books to Read:

The Maine Woods by Henry David Thoreau (Norton, 1950). A now classic account of travels in the Maine woods during the first half of the 19th century. Thoreau discusses both natural and human history of the forest.

Tall Trees, Tough Men by Robert E. Pike (Norton, 1967). A history of the lumber industry in New Hampshire.

A History of the Maine Woods by Philip T. Coolidge, privately printed, Bangor, Maine, 1963. A history of the lumber industry in Maine.

The Primeval Hardwood Forests

In 1913, New England's last large stand of primeval hardwood forest, a 300-acre tract in Colebrook, Connecticut, was cut to the ground. The most impressive feature of this forest was, of course, the size of its trees. As one might expect in a forest that has remained undisturbed for centuries, there were trees in every stage of development and decay, from seedlings to rotting logs crisscrossing the forest floor. The largest trees had trunks over 3 feet in diameter and reached a height of 110 feet. This height seems to be about the limit to which the trees in this forest tract would grow; the tallest trees had ceased to send up leaders, the vertical branch that eventually thickens into trunk, but instead became "stag headed" or bushy on top. Ring counts showed some of these trees to be 350 years old.

Over half the forest trees were hemlock and beech, with smaller percentages of yellow birch, hard maple, red oak, and others. All of the seedlings and young trees that grew in the shady forest floor were of the same species as the adults, indicating that the old forest had long since reached a climax stage.

Another unusual characteristic of this forest was the moistness of the forest floor and the luxuriant vegetation that grew there. Such shade-tolerant shrubs as mountain laurel, Canada yew, and hobblebush grew in profusion. A thick carpet of mosses covered the ground and rocks; some species of moss grew 75 feet up the trunks of the giant trees. Although ferns and herbaceous plants were common in the forest, their variety was small; only the most tolerant species could grow in the deep shade.

It is probably a misconception to think of the primeval hardwood forests, or any other forest for that matter,

Primeval forest in the Pisgah Tract,   (Photo: Harvard University)
Winchester, New Hampshire. This
photograph, taken in 1936, shows a mixed
forest of hemlocks and hardwoods. Trees
of many different sizes growing together
are characteristic of virgin forests.

as having remained static for thousands of years. When the first European settlers arrived, no doubt much of the forest, particularly away from the coast, consisted of giant trees often several hundred years old. But there were probably many additional areas in which the trees were younger, the result of natural disturbances that occurred from time to time over the years.

Since his arrival on the continent, the white man has undoubtedly been the chief agent of destruction and change in the forest. Yet, even within this time there have been many instances of natural catastrophes, mostly hurricanes and lightning-caused fires, that have damaged large areas of the forest. There is no reason to believe that similar disturbances did not occur in previous centuries.

Every century or so destructive hurricanes must have battered the primeval forest. Within historical times, in the years 1635, 1815, and 1938, hurricanes have damaged the New England forests. Skillful forest detective work has revealed destruction from an earlier storm about the year 1400.

Although the great majority of forest fires have been the result of man's carelessness, some do occur naturally. For example, in 1952 alone, lightning caused 155 of 300 forest fires in Maine. An exceptional year to be sure, but other exceptional years undoubtedly occurred before the era of modern forest fire protection. Once ignited, the forests would burn until rain extinguished them. No doubt in dry years prior to the white man's arrival, serious fires destroyed large tracts of forest.

Forest investigators doubt that devastating outbreaks of disease and insect attack similar to those of modern times occurred over widespread areas of the primeval forest. Smaller outbreaks may have occurred, however, following damage by fire or wind.

Large tracts of the New England forests were probably spared damage by natural catastrophe for centuries. These were the forests of giant trees similar to the Colebrook tract, commonly thought of as "virgin forest." But even where the forest suffered no catastrophic disturbance, a slowly changing climate over the centuries probably caused slow changes in its composition.

Fossil evidence has indicated that as the climate moderated at the end of the glacial period, the barren land was repopulated first by tundra plants, then spruce, then northern hardwoods, and finally in southern and central New England by oak and hickory. Much of this change was no doubt caused by the climatic requirements of the different species. Spruce, for example, could withstand the rigors of the harsh climate near the margins of the melting ice, but as the climate moderated other trees gradually moved northward to compete successfully with and gradually replace it.

Slow climatic changes are still going on. Evidence suggests that about 2,000 years ago New England had a climate that was, on the average, somewhat warmer and drier than it is today. During the time that has elapsed since then there have been at least local changes in the composition of the forests. Just how widespread these changes have been, however, is not clear; but the idea of "the virgin forest," a woodland tract whose composition of tree species remained unchanged for century after century, is probably incorrect.

During the 1800s there were still large areas of primeval forest left in central and northern New England, but with the invention of the steam sawmill and the advance of the railroads into heretofore inaccessible areas, these forests were quickly consumed. Although there are still a few tracts of primeval spruce forest remaining in New England, practically every acre of the hardwood forest had been cut before anyone realized that preserving a few undisturbed stands might be of some practical value. Aside from their beauty and purely scientific interest, primeval forests, where natural reforestation had been proceeding for centuries, offered clues to proper forest management.

After the destruction of the Colebrook tract, all that remained was a few acres of primeval hardwood forest in southwestern New Hampshire. In 1927 Harvard University was given 20 acres of virgin timber on Mt. Pisgah, a hill near the town of Winchester, New Hampshire, for study by its Forestry School. In the ensuing years Harvard personnel studied the various habitats in the forest and gathered substantial data on the number, size, and age of the trees, as well as evidence of past disturbance. On September 21, 1938, their studies came to an abrupt end when the disastrous hurricane roared up the Connecticut Valley and almost completely leveled the forest.

The composition of this forest varied somewhat from place to place. As in the Colebrook tract, hemlock was one of the common trees, but here the other most common tree was white pine, not beech. The white pines were true giants ranging up to 150 feet in height with trunks 4 feet in diameter. The hardwoods that also grew here were typical of this forest region. They included red oak, beech, black birch, paper birch, and maple, in that order of abundance. Counts of the tree rings showed that some of the hemlocks were almost 400 years old and the white pines and hardwoods about 250 years old.

In comparison to the present-day northern hardwood forests, the estimated volume of timber on this virgin tract was fantastic. About 33,000 board feet per acre was the average of the whole 20-acre tract, about 10 times as much as the estimated average volume of today's northern woodlands. Thirty-three thousand board feet was only the average; on some acre tracts the volume

*The Pisgah Tract after the 1938 hurricane.
This disastrous hurricane almost
completely leveled New England's last
stand of virgin timber and did millions of
dollars' worth of damage to forests
elsewhere.*

(*Photo:* Harvard University)

was much higher, up to an incredible 85,000 board feet. Such high-yield acreage, however, was largely forested by white pine.

Old timber records have yielded information about the vanished primeval forests in other parts of New England. In northern New England, probably because of the shorter growing season, the hardwood forests were not so impressive. In Maine, for example, the virgin hardwoods were only "two log" trees, that is, each tree yielded only two 16-foot logs of clear timber. By comparison, the Colebrook trees in south-central New England probably yielded three or perhaps even four 16-foot logs. Of course, virgin white pine often grew half again as tall as the tallest hardwoods.

Many people have come to realize the desirability of preserving tracts of undisturbed forest. As a consequence, in each of the New England states there are now areas owned either by the state or by a conservation organization, that will remain undisturbed in perpetuity. Some of these tracts already support impressive stands of timber.

With present-day methods of fire and insect protection, many of these may grow to duplicate the primeval forest that doubtless covered much of New England. But trees grow slowly. It may be another century or two before New England once again has stands of forest similar to the primeval forests that greeted the first settlers.

A Place to Visit:

Gifford Woods State Park, Sherburne, Vt. (USGS Rutland) includes a 5 acre tract of primeval northern hardwood forest. One tree over 400 years old.

The White Pine

On a hillside just south of the village of Cornwall in northwestern Connecticut, there grows what is probably the most magnificent stand of white pine in New England. Many of these trees — which are known as the "Cathedral Pines" — top 150 feet in height; laid end to end two of these trees would stretch the length of a football field. Significantly, however, growing in the deep shade cast by these giants are not young pines, but a rising generation of hemlock, beech, and maple. So when the tall pines finally die, the next forest that grows on that Connecticut hillside will be far different from the Cathedral Pines of today.

During the nineteenth century, New England's agriculture had reached its high water mark and started to decline. All across New England thousands of square miles of land had been cleared, farmed for a time, then abandoned. Pine is a sun-loving tree. The newly abandoned fields provided a natural nursery for pines. The light, paper-thin seeds shed from the cones of older pines growing in the neighborhood drifted into the fields, where they germinated in the grass. Within a few years after the farmer mowed his field for the last time, there would be a vigorous stand of young pines growing there. Through competition, the trees would naturally thin themselves out as they grew taller. Within 50 years, in place of an old field there would be a grove of tall, straight pines.

By the turn of the century there were so many pines growing in central New England that the first people to study the New England woodlands designated the central area as the "White Pine Region." Practically all of the pine forests were growing in abandoned fields.

After the widespread cutting of the old field pine, the forest once more returned to hardwoods. Young pines could rarely grow in the deep shade cast by the parent trees. On the other hand, shade-tolerant hardwoods could. By the time mature pines were felled, there was usually a stand of hardwood saplings growing in the shady understory. With the canopy removed, these young hardwoods made a spurt of growth and in turn shaded out any pine seedlings that might have germinated. As a consequence, the woodlands, once mainly pine, reverted back to hardwoods.

The white pine has played an important role in both New England's history and its economy. The early colonists could not have found a more suitable wood with which to build their settlements. The pines were large, their wood straight-grained, durable, and light. Pine wood was equally well suited for cabinetry or house construction. Many fine examples of colonial pine furniture and houses survive to this day.

The British Admiralty recognized the value of white pine for masts and spars. In 1688, a king's decree reserved all suitable pines with trunk diameters of 24 inches or more for the Royal Navy. All of the mast pines were stamped with a broad arrow signifying these trees to be crown property. The broad arrow policy was a source of irritation to the colonists right up until the Revolution, but apparently they obeyed the decree, for it is almost impossible to find 24-inch pine planks in any of the houses built during the colonial times, although 22- and 23-inch planks are common.

The mast pines were first cut in the vicinity of rivers, where they could be floated to settlements near the coast and thence sent by ship to England. But soon the supply near the rivers became exhausted. By 1700, pine masts were being cut 20 miles from the nearest river. Dragging a log, often 100 feet long and 3 feet wide at the butt, through 20 miles of trackless forest would be a major undertaking even today; in those days with only oxen and primitive sleds, it must have been a tremendous task, probably requiring many days.

Early accounts such as this have led forest biologists to believe that white pine was not nearly as common then as it is today. In fact, the Reverend Timothy Dwight, an early president of Yale, writing at the end of the 1700s, estimated that all the pine woods in New England could easily fit into one Connecticut county. A century later, old field white pine became one of rural New England's greatest sources of wealth.

Before the temporary nature of the pine forests was clearly understood, many landowners tried to reforest cut over areas with white pine, hoping that eventually a second crop of this valuable tree could be harvested. Most of these attempts were complete failures. It was only through constant cutting of the hardwood saplings surrounding the pines that the young trees could receive enough light to grow. Even in spite of these efforts, the second growth was often spindly and diseased.

Yet white pine would occasionally reseed itself naturally. The trees had managed to survive for thousands of years before the colonists arrived, but apparently they grew more often as single, isolated trees rather than in thick stands. The studies of the virgin forest at the Pisgah tract indicated that white pine might be able to compete successfully with the shade-tolerant hardwoods on dry, sandy, and exposed sites, so that in some places white pine might represent a forest climax tree.

White pine, like most other trees, has its serious enemies. The worst of these is the white pine blister rust. Like several other serious tree diseases, the blister rust was a European import, coming in with some nursery stock from France about 1905. The rust fungus needs two hosts to complete its life cycle: the white pine and the wild currant or gooseberry. From the gooseberry or currant, the fungus spreads to the white pine, causing an outbreak of blisters on branches. These eventually spread downward and girdle the trunk. The blisters destroy the living layer of inner bark and the result is just as disastrous to the tree as if it had been girdled with an ax.

The disease immediately created a serious problem. Instead of merely infecting trees nearby, the spores were often blown to other trees several miles away. Once the role of the gooseberries in the transmission of blister rust was discovered, foresters could control the disease by rooting out this alternate host to the rust fungus. Where this has been done, there has been a good measure of control of the blister rust.

The 1938 hurricane toppled pines by the thousands. Although the virgin pines on the Pisgah tract caught the full force of the hurricane and were leveled, in most areas it was the younger, second-growth pines that took the worst beatings. These young pines had more limbs for their size than did the old growth; in addition they usually lacked the extensive root system that the older trees had developed over the years. Often the pines at the outer edges of the grove, those whose root systems had developed in response to ordinary windstorms, survived while the more sheltered pines in the middle fell.

The New England timber industry — its mainstay being white pine — never really recovered from the 1938 hurricane. For several decades prior to the hurricane, many land owners had been managing their pine forests to increase their yield of saw timber, weeding out inferior trees, thinning the pines to eliminate wasteful competition, even pruning off lower branches to improve the quality of timber by eliminating knots. In a single afternoon many people saw years of work destroyed as their pine forests toppled. The hurricane destroyed faith in big trees as an investment; few people are now willing to grow saw timber in their forests. Pulpwood from half-grown trees is more certain, brings a quicker return, and requires no management. Thus, most privately-owned New England forests will remain immature and even-aged, being periodically cut over before the trees can reach any great size.

Although white pine is found growing naturally in almost all parts of New England, it is most common in the central regions. There are still stands of large trees that survived the hurricane throughout the regions, but probably all of these — even the 200-year-old trees in Cornwall, Connecticut — represent second growth in once-cleared land. Several of the more prominent stands of large pines are listed below.

Places to Visit:

Cathedral Pines, Cornwall, Conn. (USGS Cornwall). .5 mile south of Cornwall Village. See description in text.

College Woods, University of New Hampshire, Durham (USGS Dover West). Survivors of a grove of 300-year-old pines and hemlock largely destroyed by the 1938 hurricane.

Carlisle Pines, Carlisle, Mass. (USGS Westford). Entrance at end of Forest Park Road off Curve Street. About two dozen enormous trees, all that remains of an extensive grove also destroyed by the 1938 hurricane.

The Gold Pines, Housatonic Forest, Cornwall, Conn. (USGS Cornwall). Unmarked entrance on south side of Route 128 about one mile east of West Cornwall covered bridge. Forty acres of old-growth pines.

Other large pine groves grow in Hanover, New Hampshire, on land owned by Dartmouth College; in Brunswick, Maine, just off the Bowdoin College campus; and in South Burlington, Vermont on land owned by the University of Vermont.

The American Chestnut

In previous sections we have seen how spruce, beech, birch, and pine each in turn have suffered very serious damage from fungus or insect attacks. But the greatest disaster of all was the fungus blight that destroyed the American chestnut.

The chestnut was probably New England's most valuable hardwood tree. It grew fast; 100-foot trees were not unusual in the hardwood forest. The wood was so resistant to decay that it was almost the exclusive choice for telephone poles and railroad ties. The nuts were valuable as a wildlife forage and a fall delicacy for city and country dwellers alike.

Chestnut was a very common tree. Across much of its range, which included most of the eastern third of the United States, chestnut vied with various species of oak for dominance of the forest. Many farmers spared the trees when clearing pasture or culling the woodland tracts for firewood. As a result, groves of chestnut trees were common on hilly pasture land. In Connecticut, forest ecologists estimate that this single species accounted for over half of the standing timber. That was before the blight struck.

The disease apparently entered the country in 1890 on some infected nursery trees brought into New York

Stump of American chestnut tree, Harvard, Massachusetts. A fungus blight introduced in 1904 has virtually wiped out one of America's most valuable trees. Still standing some 40 years after the blight killed it, this tree demonstrates the decay-resistance of chestnut wood. Scale is shown by the author's young son.

City from China. By 1904 the epidemic had been identified, but a curious combination of circumstances — inaction by the New York State legislators and public apathy — prevented any measures to control the disease while the epidemic was still localized. The blight radiated from New York like spokes on a wheel. The chestnuts had no natural resistance and died by the thousands. Traveling from tree to tree at a speed of 20 miles per year, the blight wiped out virtually all of the chestnuts in New England before 1920 and reached the last of the trees in the Great Smoky Mountains by the 1940s. Only one small colony in Michigan, far enough removed from the rest, has thus far escaped destruction.

Though no longer a forest tree of any importance, the chestnut has not yet disappeared. Young trees are blight-resistant for a time. In woodlands where the chestnut was a common tree, young chestnuts still sprout from the living roots of the older trees. Often young chestnut sprouts are among the most common trees in the understory. But as they grow and approach flowering and fruiting maturity and the bark begins to furrow, tell-tale orange fans of the blight fungus almost invariably appear on their trunks. The blight penetrates the inner bark layers and quickly kills the tree. Then the fungus releases windborne spores that drift on to the young trees nearby.

A tiny fraction of the American chestnut trees may remain blight resistant to maturity, but resistance seems to be a genetic trait linked to undesirable characteristics. Resistant trees are almost always spindly, rendering them unfit for timber as well as poor nut producers. What is more, these trees do not pass blight resistance on to the offspring, at least not to the first generation.

Because chestnut wood is so resistant to decay, many New England woodlands are still littered with dead trees. When the blight struck, the landowners cut most of the salable timber, but those trees that were too small or too short-trunked to be of much value remained. The smaller trees have almost all fallen and now crisscross the forest floors. But some of the larger ones are still standing some 50 years after their death. These old hulks, now shorn of their limbs and bleached by the weather, are the last remnants of a once valuable forest tree.

Recently, however, investigators at the Connecticut Agricultural field station have discovered a promising treatment for the blight-ridden American Chestnut tree. Inoculation with a non-virulent strain of the fungus has resulted in a remission of the blight symptoms on infected trees and, thus far, recurrence of the disease. Even if this treatment should prove permanently effective on individual trees, it is still problematical whether it could be employed on a scale that would return the species to its former dominant state. Nevertheless, it seems to be a major breakthrough in controlling the fungus and one that may enable future generations of New Englanders to appreciate and enjoy these beautiful trees.

A Book to Read:

Connecticut Hybrid Chestnuts and Their Culture, Bulletin 657, by Richard A. Jaynes and Arthur H. Graves (The Connecticut Agricultural Experiment Station, New Haven, 1963). Describes work being done to produce a hybrid blight-resistant chestnut tree suitable for New England. (Out of Print)

The Oak-Hickory Forest

The typical upland forests of southern New England have a different appearance from the northern hardwood forests. First, the trees themselves are different. Here oaks are the most common trees; their lustrous dark green leaves provide a sharp contrast to the delicate greens of the northern hardwoods. Hickory and red maple are also common trees on drier sites.

Where there is a bit more moisture, the variety of trees increases. Not only do the northern hardwood trees still appear occasionally, but a number of southern trees including black birch, sweet gum (in southwestern Connecticut), tulip tree, and dogwood join the tree community. In extreme southern New England, however, hemlock and the northern hardwoods become limited to shady ravines and moist, north-facing slopes. White pine, so common in central New England, also becomes scarce in the extreme southern part.

The oak forests in southern New England also appear drier and more open than those of the north. In place of the lush undergrowth of the northern forest, large patches of the forest floor are entirely bare of vegetation or support only monotonous growth of blueberry, sheep laurel, or huckleberry. Generally speaking, the southern woods are drier than those farther north. Although both areas receive about the same yearly rainfall, the hot sun and longer summer season dries out the southern woods more rapidly. Where some ground water is available, however, the southern New England woods support thick undergrowth.

Another characteristic of the southern New England woodlands is the relatively small size of the trees. The miles of stone walls that crisscross the woods point out how much of the land was once cleared; most of these woodlands date from the turn of the century or later. Small trees fail to provide the thick, leafy canopy that retards evaporation, and this also contributes to the dryness of the southern woodlands.

Coppice trees — that is, trees with several trunks growing in a clump from one set of roots — are a common sight in the oak-hickory forest. Oaks, hickories, and several other hardwoods that are common in these woodlands have the ability to send up sprouts from burned or cut stumps. Although one set of roots can support several generations of trees, the later generations are almost always several-trunked coppice trees. The trunks are usually bent or crowded, the wood unfit for timber. So common are these sprouted, second-growth trees that the oak-hickory region is sometimes referred to as the "sprout hardwoods" region.

The majority of young trees and stump sprouts point to the tremendous influence of man upon these woodlands. It is clear that most of the forests are still in the process of renewal from large-scale disturbances that have taken place since the arrival of the first European settlers about 350 years ago.

But man's disturbance of these southern New England forests began long before the coming of the Europeans. Some ecologists believe that the effects of nearly 10,000 years of Indian occupancy accounts in large measure for the present-day distribution of trees. Radiocarbon dating has established that Indians lived in coastal Massachusetts at least 9,000 years ago. This date may be conservative, for radiocarbon dating has indicated that Indians were living in New York State over 3,000 years before that. By the time the first Europeans arrived, there was a flourishing Indian culture all up and down the New England coast and on several of the larger rivers. An early estimate puts the Indian population as high as 80,000.

These Indians lived in more or less permanent settlements where they cleared land and farmed it. The first Europeans found large tracts of cleared land all along the coast. In fact, the area around Boston was reported to be so free of forest, presumably cleared by the Indians, that the early settlers had to cut their firewood from the islands in the harbor.

Following the practice of many aboriginal people, the Indians cleared their land by burning it; no doubt they unintentionally started forest fires as well. The seriousness of these fires and the damage caused by them of course depended on how dry the woodlands were. Undoubtedly most of the fires were merely ground fires that kept the underbrush in check, encouraged the growth of grass, but did little damage to the mature trees. Occasionally, however, these Indian fires must have been wholesale conflagrations, consuming the trees and burning until rain extinguished them. Several accounts of the explorers and early settlers mention palls of smoke from these Indian fires visible for many miles.

There is a marked difference among biologists as to whether this burning, that must have occurred over thousands of years, had any long-term effects on the tree community that are still visible today. One group believes that it has. They point out that the distribution of the oak-hickory forest along southern and coastal New England coincides with the probable centers of the Indian population.

Continual burning would favor the sprout hardwoods — oaks, hickories, and red maple — over those hardwoods that lacked the ability to sprout after fire. This group of biologists also points to the rarity of conifers in these southern forests. Conifers are initially more flammable and also lack the ability to sprout from stumps. Pitch pine, the only conifer common in the southern New England woodlands, has fire-resistant cones and often reseeds burned areas. These biologists note that the only places where hemlock and the more fire-sensitive hardwoods grow are in moist sites that would have afforded some natural protection from fire. They predict that hemlock, because of its longevity and extreme shade-tolerance, will gradually increase to become the major climax tree in the oak-hickory forest, now that the dangers of fire have lessened.

Another group of biologists look at the same distribution of trees in the oak-hickory region and reach different conclusions. Fire, they argue, was not common or widespread enough in the pre-colonial forests to cause any long-term change in the tree community. This group believes that the dry, warm climate of southern New England was what favored the oak and hickory. They point out that the appearance of the few mature stands of today's oak-hickory forest closely fit the early explorers' description of the pre-colonial forest as being open and park-like, through which a man could easily ride on horseback. This group believes that the present climate in southern New England is too warm and dry for hemlock ever to venture far beyond the moist shady sites where it presently grows, and thus hemlock will never compete with oak and hickory as the common climax tree on the drier uplands.

The problem is far from being settled. Both groups can marshal evidence to support their positions, but none of it is really conclusive. Perhaps we must wait until the woodlands slowly mature before the controversy will be settled.

Because of the long history of settlement in southern New England, the oak-hickory region, practically no stands of old-growth timber remain. In Stonington, Connecticut, one 40-acre fragment of oak-hickory forest approaching primeval condition survived until the 1938 hurricane, but forest biologists who studied this tract both before and after its destruction doubted that the trees were truly virgin timber. The tree community at Stonington was similar to the second-growth forests in the region; oak, hickory, and red maple were common trees. In contrast to the primeval stands of northern hardwood forests, the trees in this forest were mostly under 2 feet in diameter. The underbrush was mostly blueberry, huckleberry, and hazelnut, common forest shrubs in dry habitats. Although the Stonington forest, because of its exposed situation along the coast, may not have been a typical representative of the primeval oak-hickory forest, this description — except for the size of its trees — is similar to that of the present-day upland forest in southern New England.

The line between the oak-hickory forests and the northern hardwoods region is indistinct. The two meet and blend together along an irregular band stretching from northwestern Connecticut to southern Maine, forming what foresters call the "transition forest." The oaks are generally southern trees, but persist in the woodlands up the Connecticut and Merrimack Valleys deep into the hardwood regions.

It may be a century or more before the southern New England woodlands reach a size to be of much value. In Rhode Island, for example, a woodland survey conducted in the 1940s showed that 30 percent of the trees in the woodlands of the state were still too small even to be of use for firewood; only 1 percent of the trees were large enough for saw timber, and these few were too widely scattered to be of any real economic value. No doubt the situation has improved somewhat in the last 20 years, but oak and hardwoods grow slowly. In addition, most of the older trees are coppices that rarely yield salable timber.

Nevertheless, all of the states have natural woodland areas that, barring fire or hurricane, will eventually return to a primeval state. These are either part of the state park systems or are owned by private organizations such as the Audubon Society or Nature Conservancy. Many already support mature woodland that can probably give visitors at least an approximate idea of the natural vegetation of this region.

Places to Visit:

Harvard Forest, Petersham, Mass. (USGS Athol). Headquarters of Harvard University Forestry School. Old growth transition forest. Small forestry museum including a series of dioramas showing the evolution of the central New England forest since the 17th century.

Hardwood Forest, Durham, N.H. (USGS Durham). Small section of transition forest on Great Bay. Detailed directions available from Dept. of Botany, University of New Hampshire, Durham. Common trees are hard maple, oak, hickory, and others. Striking wildflower display in April

Algonquin State Forest, Colebrook, Conn. (USGS Winsted). Off Route 8 north of Robertsville. Exceptionally beautiful example of mature transition woodland. Portions of the forest set aside as wilderness preserve.

James L. Goodwin State Forest and *Conservation Center,* Hampton, Conn. (USGS Hampton). North side of Route 6, one mile east of Clark's Corner. Example of controlled conservation and woodland management.

Old-growth forest on Governor's Island in Pine Acres Lake has some of the largest trees in the oak-hickory region. Adjoins the *Natchaug State Forest* on the north.

Sleeping Giant State Park, Hamden, Conn. (USGS Wallingford & Mt. Carmel). One of the typical basalt ridges of the Connecticut Lowland. Route 10, north of Mt. Carmel. Beautiful woodlands. Nature trail. Twenty-seven miles of trails.

Pachaug State Forest, Voluntown, Conn. (USGS Voluntown). Largest state forest in Connecticut. Forest nursery off Sheldon Road near Glasco Pond. Also see p. 125 and p. 220 for other points of interest in this forest.

White Memorial Foundation, Litchfield, Conn. (USGS Litchfield). Bissell Road off Route 25 one mile northeast of Bantam. Nature Center and Museum. Managed forests. Experimental grove of blight resistant chestnut trees.

Dead Creek Oak Hickory Woods, Addison, Vt. (USGS Port Henry, N.Y.–Vt.) privately owned tract of oak hickory woods in the Champlain region of Northwestern Vermont.

Books to Read:

Yale Natural Preserve, New Haven, and *The Natural Area of the Audubon Center of Greenwich* by Frank E. Egler and William A. Niering (State Geological and Natural History Survey of Connecticut, 1966). First two volumes in a series on the vegetation of Connecticut natural areas. Description of the forest ecology in areas that are being kept free from human interference. Very useful guides. Several additional volumes are in preparation. (Available from State Librarian, 25¢ each.)

Connecticut Walk Book (Connecticut Forest and Park Association, 1968). Complete guide to Connecticut's extensive trail system. (Available from Conn. Forest and Park Association or Appalachian Mountain Club, $3.50.)

Connecticut Outdoor Recreation Guide (Connecticut Forest and Park Association, 1968). Complete listing of all parks and natural areas owned by the state and nonprofit organizations. Excellent guide. (Available from Conn. Forest and Park Association.)

Short Walks in Connecticut, 3 volumes, by Eugene Keyarts (Pequot Press, 1973). Excellent pocket guides to 125 country walks in Connecticut. Easy to follow maps.

Fifty Hikes in Massachusetts by Paul and Ruth Sadlier. (New Hampshire Publishing Co., Somersworth, N.H., 1975.) Informative guide to 50 day hikes. Maps, text, photographs.

A.M.C. Massachusetts–Rhode Island Trail Guide, 3rd Ed. (Appalachian Mountain Club, 1977). Guide to hikes of all kinds, from short walks to wilderness journeys.

Short Walks on Cape Cod and the Vineyard by Ruth & Paul Sadlier (Pequot Press, 1976). Fine pocket guide, good photographs and maps.

The Woodland Shrubs and Herbs

Thus far, little mention has been given to the shrubs and herbs of New England's woodlands. These smaller members of the forest community have an even more sporadic distribution than do the trees. Anyone who has done much walking in the woods has probably found areas where the ground is literally carpeted with a great variety and abundance of flowering plants and shrubs, while in a seemingly identical habitat nearby there will be only last year's crop of tree leaves on the forest floor. Because their populations vary so greatly even within similar habitats, as well as from one habitat to another, it makes little sense to list or describe even the most common plants one is likely to encounter in the woods. Sometimes they will be there, other times not.

Instead, it might be more useful to discuss some of the ecological factors that seem to influence the distribution of the woodland plants and shrubs, and let the reader, armed with this information, plus good wildflower and shrub guides, make his own list of the plants growing in the woods he explores.

The same natural factors that determine the distribution of trees have an even greater effect on the shrubs and plants. On one hand there are the constraints put on the distribution of shrubs and plants by regional differences in climate, usually manifested by winter temperatures and length of growing season; on the other, there are the local factors such as moisture, light, and soil acidity that determine the habitat. Because plants have evolved to grow in almost every conceivable habitat, however, no general statements about their distribution and ecology will apply to every species. Moreover, the distribution of individual species does not always conform to man-made rules; these smaller members of the forest community, like the trees themselves, often turn up in habitats where they are least expected. With these warnings in mind, then, we will examine some of the natural factors that influence the distribution of shrubs and plants in the forest.

Moisture is a far more crucial problem for most of these smaller members of the forest community than it is for trees. Although, like trees, different plant and shrub species have differing moisture requirements, their shallow root systems and small size make many of them sensitive to drought. It is almost always possible to find a greater abundance and variety of plants and shrubs in more moist habitats.

The types of trees that are growing in the woodland will also affect the availability of moisture to the plants. Ash, maple, and elm all have surface-feeding roots that draw moisture away from the plants. Oaks and hickories, on the other hand, have much deeper root systems that don't compete so vigorously with shallow-rooted plants and shrubs.

Surprisingly enough, light is another factor that affects the variety of plant life on the forest floor. Most plants and shrubs, normally thought of as enjoying a woodland habitat, will spread and blossom more profusely where they receive some light. This is one reason why country roadsides usually have more wildflowers growing there than do the adjacent woods. Selective cutting that thins the tree canopy often produces a marked increase in the shrubs and plants. Clear cutting, on the other hand, causes such a drastic increase in sunlight that few of the delicate woodland plants can survive. Moreover, the sunny environment of a cut-over woodland encourages the invasion of a number of vigorous, sun-loving plants such as grasses and raspberries that often crowd out most woodland plants that otherwise might have survived.

Only a relatively small number of plants and shrubs can survive in the deep shade of the primeval forest. In the tract at Colebrook, Connecticut, for example, the 300-acre area supported only 10 shrub species and 60 different plants and ferns, a smaller number than is likely to be found in the average vacant lot.

Soil acidity is another crucial factor for some plants. Generally, a neutral or only slightly acidic soil provides the optimum conditions for most plants. Strongly acidic soils, the type that occur in bogs, are toxic to all but a few plants; at the other end of the scale, strongly alkaline soils also support a limited flora, although these soils are limited mostly to desert areas and do not occur in the humid climate of New England except directly adjacent to limestone or marble.

The type of underlying bedrock is an important determinant of soil acidity. In areas underlain by limestone, the subsoil, at least, is usually neutral or slightly alkaline. The limy subsoil has the same effect on the trees as ground limestone has on a lawn or garden. Limestone is not primarily a fertilizer, but by neutralizing the soil it hastens decay of organic matter and aids plants by liberating minerals that otherwise would remain locked in the soil. Small amounts of calcium, one of the components of limestone, are also required by most plants.

The principal areas in New England where the underlying rock is limestone, or a related alkaline rock, are the Valley of Vermont and its southern extension into Massachusetts, the Champlain Lowland, and northeastern Maine. Several smaller limestone areas occur elsewhere.

*Maidenhair spleenwort, Bartholomew's
Cobble, Ashley Falls, Massachusetts.
A small, rock-loving fern whose
presence almost always indicates
the presence of limestone or other
calcareous rock.*

A glance at the distribution maps for tree species shows that several of these extend their range northward into these limestone regions. In addition, a number of tree species form disjunct colonies beyond the northern limit of their range in regions where the soil is less acidic. There may be other ecological factors at work here, but we might infer that the more hospitable growing conditions offered by the soil more than offset the harsher northern climate.

The trees themselves affect the soil acidity. Oak leaves contain *tannin,* an acid compound, that tends to retard decomposition. As a result, oak woods, like those growing conifers, tend to have acidic forest soils. We have seen, on the other hand, that the northern hardwood leaves decay rapidly and tend to produce a neutral topsoil.

There are a number of native plants, such as blueberry and mountain laurel, that cannot tolerate lime; they occur naturally in limestone areas only where a thick layer of acidic forest mold insulates their roots from contact with the rock. Likewise, there are a number of other plants, including several small, rock-loving ferns, that are almost always associated with limestone. Their presence in a region is almost a certain indication that the bedrock contains a significant amount of lime.

Man's disruption of the forests has had a tremendous influence on the distribution of woodland plants and shrubs. When a woodland is heavily lumbered or cleared, whole populations of plants that depend on the shade and moisture of the woodlands are wiped out. In addition, most of the shallow-rooted, smaller members of the forest community are completely destroyed by burning. Lowbush blueberry seems to be one of the few shrubs that can survive fire.

When one considers how populations of these woodland plants and shrubs must have been decimated by the widespread clearing of the land in southern New England during the 1800s, it seems surprising that the young woodlands of today contain as many different plants as they do. It is important to remember that the geographical range of a particular plant, rooted to the ground as it is, is zero. If its habitat becomes unsuitable, the plant dies. Extension from one habitat to another, therefore, depends wholly on the chance dispersal of seeds into a suitable spot to germinate and grow. Practically all of the plants in today's woodlands of southern New England have radiated outward from the few woodland refuges that managed to survive the agricultural boom.

The widespread clearing of the land, on the other hand, encouraged some flowering plants that could not stand shade or strong competition with other plants. Fifty years ago, for example, a small orchid, arethusa, was a common spring flower in wet meadows; the bright blue fringed gentian was equally common in the fall. As the fields have been returning to forest, both of these flowers have become increasingly rare.

Another plant that has increased tremendously in the last 75 years is poison ivy. Apparently the widespread clearing of the land was initially responsible for its spread, but during this time grazing held it in check. As farming declined and the land was abandoned, this noxious pest spread rampantly through pasture and woodland, rendering large tracts of land in southern New England completely impassable. Poison ivy has established itself as a permanent ground cover; in many places it forms such dense thickets that it overwhelms most of the more desirable shrubs and plants. Since very few people are immune to its poison, it is well for anyone who walks in the woods to learn to recognize this rank-growing vine. Its most easily identifiable characteristics are shiny leaves borne in groups of three.

In addition to causing drastic changes in the populations of the native plants, man has introduced a large number of European plants that have become thoroughly naturalized. Almost one-fifth of New England's wild plants are European imports that have been introduced since colonial times. Such common plants as ragweed, daisies, dandelions, and nearly 1,000 others are naturalized imports, mostly from Europe.

Several of the more serious weed pests were deliberately imported by New England residents as garden flowers. The devil's paintbrush, a small weed whose orange, dandelion-like flowers are now a common sight in fields and pastures, was a garden flower that aggressively spread to the fields and pastures. Another garden escapee, purple loosestrife, is one of the most common marsh plants in New England. Anyone who has driven around the eastern and southern part of the region in late summer cannot help but notice the magenta-pink spikes of loosestrife, sometimes covering whole acres of wet meadows and marshland. The weed is so aggressive and rampant that it often forms pure stands crowding out all other plants. Fifty years ago purple loosestrife was a rarity in New England.

Books to Read:

The Study of Plant Communities by Henry J. Oosting (W. H. Freeman and Co., San Francisco, 1948). Excellent introduction to plant ecology. Emphasis on eastern United States.

Plant Communities by Rexford Daubenmire (Harper and Row, 1968). Another fine ecology text. Emphasis on western United States.

Forest Ecology by Stephan Spurr. See description, page 145.

The Deciduous Forests of Eastern North America by E. Lucy Braun. See description, page 145.

Reading the Landscape by May Theilgaard Watts. See description, page 178.

The Plants of the Heath Family

Of the many plant families represented in the understory of New England woodlands, the heath family stands preeminent. The name "heath" tells little about the American members of this family. Heaths are shrubby plants that grow on British moorland; none grow naturally in the Western Hemisphere. If instead this family were named the "azalea family" or the "blueberry family" after two of its more common American members, most people would immediately recognize it, and many could name a few other shrubs and plants that belong there. The heath family includes many common woodland plants as well as a number of other decorative species which, though not native, grow in New England gardens.

In the northeast, azalea, rhododendron, and mountain laurel are the best known members of the heath family. All three are native to New England, although rhododendrons grow naturally in only a few places. Of the other two, mountain laurel is the more common.

Abundant in many parts of southern and central New England, mountain laurel thrives in the dappled shade and acid soil beneath oak trees. It is one of the most easily recognized of all woodland shrubs. Its dark green shining leaves remain on the plant through the winter; in June, clusters of white to pink flowers adorn it. In congenial habitats, mountain laurel will grow up to 15 feet high. It is most abundant in the stony upland soils on the high ground east of the Connecticut Valley, but it is locally common on the west side as well. Although mountain laurel is highly regarded by most people, in some parts of New England it forms such dense thickets that local residents look upon it as a weed. Why they call these thickets "laurel hells" becomes abundantly clear to anybody attempting to walk through one.

Most botanists regard azaleas as part of the rhododendron genus, but for the layman enough superficial differences exist between the two to render each distinct. Although New England has not nearly the variety of azaleas the southern Appalachians have, there are four native species that brighten the bogs and woodlands with their spring flowers. No doubt the best known of these is the little bog azalea, rhodora. Its reddish-purple blossoms are among the first spring flowers to appear in the cold and soggy spruce bogs. Less well known but more common are mountain azalea (*Rhododendron roseum*) and pinxter flower (*R. nudiflorum*). The two look quite similar but the blossoms of the more northern mountain azalea have a spicy clovelike fragrance. As its name implies, the swamp white azalea (*R. viscosum*) grows in swamps or wet woods. Its blossoms appear in late June or July.

The only rhododendron species — as the layman conceives of it — native to New England is the rosebay rhododendron (*R. maximum*). Although very common in the southern Appalachians, it is found in only a handful of places in New England. It grows in several of the cedar bogs of eastern Connecticut and Rhode Island, but becomes increasingly scarce northward, so scarce, in fact, that several of these isolated colonies have been set aside for preservation.

The Trustees of Reservations own one of these scattered colonies in Medfield, Massachusetts; Rhododendron State Park near Jaffrey, New Hampshire, is another; and a colony in Springvale, Maine, owned by the Wildflower Society is a third. The last of these was believed to be the most northerly rhododendron colony in New England, but recently a more northerly one was found on the slopes of Mt. Chocorua, and another growing improbably in the harsh mountain climate of King-field, Maine.

The rosebay rhododendron looks very similar to the garden varieties. It has the same oval evergreen leaves and the same clustered arrangement of its flowers. These are light pink, and appear in July. Like other wild species, rosebay rhododendron can not match the flamboyant floral display of its hybrid cousins, but, nevertheless, it is among the finest of wildflowers. It is no surprise that in the nineteenth century, before hybrids became plentiful, several of the more accessible New England colonies of this plant were transplanted for use as landscaping shrubs. Fortunately, with the great array of hybrid rhododendrons now available, the remaining colonies are less likely to become extinct.

There are many other less spectacular members of the heath family growing in New England. Blueberry and huckleberry, the ever-present shrubs of dry woodlands, are both heaths, as is sheep laurel, a poor relative of mountain laurel. Interestingly enough, sheep laurel seems equally at home in bogs or dry pastures. Other bog-dwelling heaths include labrador tea, leatherleaf, wild cranberry, and several more.

One of the best loved of all New England wildflowers, the trailing arbutus or mayflower, also belongs to this family. Shortly after the snow leaves the woods, small clusters of fragrant pink flowers appear among the leathery evergreen leaves of this trailing vine. The common habitat for trailing arbutus is moist sandy soil, usually in the vicinity of conifers. The plant ranges all across New England, becoming more common to the north. Tradition has it that the trailing arbutus was the first spring flower to greet the Puritans after that first terrible winter. The flower has been exterminated in some areas by people who tore up the vines wholesale and hawked them on the city streets for Christmas decorations. Several states now have laws that have stopped this practice.

Another common heath plant is the checkerberry or wintergreen. As its name suggests, the dark green leaves remain on the plant all winter. The tender spring growth has a spicy "wintergreen" flavor and its red berries are also edible. Like the arbutus, wintergreen prefers sandy soil.

What possible resemblance, one might ask, is there between such plants as, for example, wintergreen and azaleas? The answer is that all members of the heath family, like each of the other plant families, have similar flowers. In the slow process of evolution the vegetative characteristics of a plant will change long before the basic structure of the flowers. For example, the size of a plant, the size and shape of its leaves, even its life style — whether it manufactures its own food or lives as a parasite on other plants — will all respond to the pressures of evolution before there are radical changes in the flower. Although they have superficial differences such as size, shape, and color, the structure of the reproductive parts of the tiny bell-like wintergreen are very similar to those of the azalea and to other members of the heath family.

There is another characteristic that links the heath family together. All can survive in acidic soil. This is the environmental factor that links the blueberries and huckleberries in the dry oak woods with rhodora and labrador tea in the soggy spruce bog, that links the wintergreen growing in the deep shade of hemlocks with a little mountain rhododendron growing in the bright sun. All of these habitats have acidic soil. As a corollary to the complex physiological changes that must have occurred to enable heaths to survive in an acidic habitat, these plants are now unable to tolerate lime, the chief element in neutral or sweet soil.

Places to Visit:

Harvey Butler and William Plummer Rhododendron Sanctuary, Springvale, Maine (USGS Berwick). Route 11A, 2 miles west of Springvale. One of the northernmost stands of rhododendrons in the country. Owned by the New England Wildflower Society.

Rhododendron State Park, Fitzwilliam, N.H. (USGS Monadnock). Route 119, 2 miles west of Fitzwilliam.

Medfield Rhodedendron Reservation, Medfield, Mass. (USGS Medfield). Entrance on right side of Spring Street, about .7 mile south of Medfield Center. Owned by the Trustees of Reservations.

Elliott Laurel Reservation, Phillipston, Mass. (USGS Templeton and Athol). Off Petersham-Templeton Road just west of Queen Lake. Fine stand of mountain laurel.

Cedar Swamp, West Kingston, Rhode Island (USGS Slocum). Historic Ministerial Road bisects the swamp's extensive stand of rhododendron, mountain laurel, and Atlantic white cedar.

Leominster State Forest, Leominster, Mass. (USGS Fitchburg). Route 31. Fine stands of mountain laurel.

Arbutus Sanctuary, Winchendon, Mass. (USGS Winchendon). 2.1 miles from Route 12 on West Street. Entrance on left.

Pachaug State Forest, Voluntown, Conn. (USGS Voluntown). Rhododendron stand not far from Rangers Headquarters off Route 49 one mile north of intersection with Route 138. Another stand of rhododendron grows in the Wyassup Block of the forest near North Stonington.

Laurel Sanctuary, Nipmuck State Forest, Union, Conn. (USGS Westford). South side of Route 190 west of junction with Route 89. Other impressive stands of mountain laurel may be seen in *Platt Hill Park,* Winchester, as well as a number of other northern Connecticut parks and forests.

Books to Read:

The Laurel Book by Richard A. Jaynes (Hafner, 1975). Complete record of North American laurels beautifully illustrated. Emphasis on mountain laurel.

Cape Cod's Woodlands

Shoot Flying Hill near the town of Barnstable is the highest of several roadside rest areas along the Mid-Cape Highway. Covering the hillside and stretching off into the distance is a monotonous scrub forest of oak and pitch pine, the typical Cape Cod woodland. To understand the reason for this type of forest, one has to look no farther than the soil.

Although Cape Cod has the mildest climate in New England, any inducement this offers the plants is more than offset by the generally poor soils. We have already seen that both the form and substance of Cape Cod and its attendant islands was almost completely the result of glaciation. Shoot Flying Hill is part of the glacial moraine; the pond-studded plains that stretch away to the south of the hill are built of sand and gravel washed there from the melting ice. Almost all of Cape Cod's soil was sandy to begin with; the meltwater streams further impoverished the soil by carrying away most of the clay particles that would normally have enriched it and increased its water-holding ability. The soil that has remained is sterile and porous, offering little sustenance to plants.

As a result, Cape Cod's flora is as impoverished as its soil. Only a fraction of the plant species that grow in southern New England can tolerate the dry, sterile soils of Cape Cod. Predictably, the trees and plants that do grow here are many of the same that grow in the sandy soils of the Jersey Pine Barrens and eastern Long Island. Scrub oak and pitch pine cover mile after square mile of dry glacial hills and sandplains. Numerous forest fires and repeated cutting have left most of the hardwoods as stump sprouts — much too slow growing and unhealthy

*Dwarf oak–pitch pine forest, Marconi
Station, Cape Cod National Seashore,
Massachusetts. This scrub forest is typical
in dry, windswept areas of outer Cape
Cod. Counts of the tree rings show that
many of these trees are over 100 years
old. The white sand on the path is the
ashy layer of the underlying podzol soil.*

ever to be of any value for timber. In addition, several of the oak species indigenous to Cape Cod never grow much beyond shrub height.

Just how marginal are the conditions for growing trees in this region is clearly illustrated on Nantucket and several of the smaller islands. Cleared of their forests by the early settlers and later abandoned, much of the land on these islands still has not returned to forest, though generations have passed since the land was last used for pasture. The scrub forest is not limited entirely to Cape Cod and the islands. It extends inland across sandy regions in southeastern Massachusetts and northern Rhode Island and occurs as scattered patches on outwash plains in the Connecticut Valley and elsewhere. But nowhere does it cover such an extensive area as Cape Cod.

Like the soils of much of the spruce-fir region to the north, those beneath the scrub oak and pitch pine are podzols. Since the region has been ice free for a longer time than northern New England, the ashy gray layer is very clearly developed and thicker than that found farther north.

In the few places where the soil is better and more moisture is available, there is a richer variety to the forest. Here hickories, yellow and gray birch, sassafras, locust, and red maple join the omnipresent oaks and pines. But it is doubtful whether the dry forest that covers most of Cape Cod ever contained this variety of trees. Captain John Smith in 1602 described Cape Cod as "only a headland of high hills of sand overgrown with shrubby pines, hurts [huckleberry] and such trash," a description that well fits much of today's woodland. Of course, by the time John Smith and the other explorers had reached Cape Cod, many thousands of years of Indian occupancy had already passed. Indian fires may have had a greater effect on the flammable woodlands of Cape Cod than on those farther inland.

On Naushon Island, the largest in the island chain that trails off the southwestern spur of Cape Cod, there is a stand of virgin forest. There is no historical evidence that the tract was ever cut, and, no doubt because of its isolation from the mainland, it has been spared the frequent fires that have regularly swept across the rest of Cape Cod. Oddly enough, the virgin tract is almost entirely beech, one of the northern hardwoods. Only a few other hardwood species occasionally appear here and there. In contrast to the virgin tracts formerly found in parts of inland New England with trees in excess of 100 feet being the norm, the beeches on Naushon Island average only 30 or 40 feet in height. Probably a combination of poor soil and the almost constant wind have kept these trees relatively close to the ground.

Like the forest trees, the plants and shrubs that are adapted to life in the sterile acid soil are also limited. Predictably, many of these belong to the heath family. The same trio of heaths that grow in the dry oak-hickory woodlands — huckleberry, sheep laurel, and blueberry — are also common on Cape Cod. Another heath common to Cape Cod, but scarce elsewhere in New England, is bearberry. This small creeping shrub is at home in bright sun and the most infertile of soils; along roadcuts it forms shining dark green mats that spread across the gravelly bankings where nothing else can grow.

Wet areas on Cape Cod tend to become boggy; here the flora is also largely comprised of heaths: high bush blueberry, azalea, and cranberry. Cranberry grows so well in the Cape Cod region that it has become a multi-million-dollar industry and the region's chief agricultural crop. A great many of the natural boglands have been dredged and channeled for growing cranberries.

Although no natural stands of rhododendron have ever been found on Cape Cod, its mild climate and acid soil make moist places ideal habitats for this plant. The

Heritage Plantation in Sandwich contains a magnificent collection of rhododendrons from three continents. The collection was part of the estate of the late C. O. Dexter, a well-known rhododendron breeder who introduced several outstanding hybrids to American gardens. Mid-May is the height of the blooming season.

Two European members of the heath family, Scotch heather and heath, are both thoroughly naturalized on Nantucket's moorland. In the 1850s, so the story goes, a lady resident of the island scattered the seeds of these European plants from her carriage during rides around the island. Many of the seeds apparently fell into congenial habitats where they germinated, grew, and spread. Now their pink and purple blooms brighten large areas of Nantucket in late summer. In connection with the failure of natural reforestation on Nantucket, it is interesting to note that in Europe the presence of heath and heather usually indicates an uncongenial habitat for trees.

Holly is another plant that has attracted the attention of Cape Cod horticulturists and plant breeders. There are several species of holly that range across New England, but the American holly, familiar in Christmas decorations, grows naturally only along the region's southern coast, reaching the northern limit of its range just below Boston. Although common across much of the southern United States, holly in New England, like rhododendron, occurs only in widely scattered colonies, but, unlike rhododendron, it does grow naturally here and there on Cape Cod.

There are two holly preserves on Cape Cod. The first of these is the Ashumet Holly Reservation near Falmouth. Now owned by the Massachusetts Audubon Society, the Ashumet Reservation was the plant breeding grounds of the late Wilfred Wheeler, a horticulturist who collected native trees and from these bred a number of strains of holly that combined beauty with hardiness. Most of the holly used in New England landscaping came from Wheeler's stock. Dogwoods, magnolias, rhododendrons, and several other species of plants and shrubs uncommon to Cape Cod also grow here. Close by, in the town of Mashpee, is the Lowell Holly Reservation. This preserve, owned by the Trustees of Reservations, contains over 300 holly trees as well as a number of other introduced and native plants.

Places to Visit:

Cape Cod National Seashore, Visitor's Center, Route 6, Eastham, Mass. Several excellent self-guiding nature trails. Most noteworthy is the Cedar Swamp Trail at the Marconi Station.

Wellfleet Bay Wildlife Sanctuary, Wellfleet, Mass. (US GS Orleans & Wellfleet). Route 6, 3.5 miles north of National Seashore Visitor's Center. Sanctuary entrance on left. Excellent self-guiding nature trails.

Ashumet Holly Reservation, Falmouth, Mass. (USGS Falmouth). Route 151, East Falmouth. See description in text.

Lowell Holly Reservation, Mashpee, Mass. (USGS Sandwich & Cotuit). Sandwich Road from Mashpee Center, left on dirt road. See description in text.

Heritage Plantation, Sandwich, Mass. (USGS Sandwich). See description in text.

Cape Cod Museum of Natural History, Brewster, Mass.

From Field to Forest

One of the most familiar scenes in New England's hill country is that of fields and pastures returning to woods. There is so much abandoned farmland in southern and central New England that it is usually possible, within the space of a few miles, to find examples of old field succession at every stage of the way — from weedy fields only recently abandoned to mature forests where a crisscrossing network of stone walls provides the only clue that the land was not always wooded.

Like other types of botanical succession, the change from field to forest often seems to follow distinct stages. In formerly cultivated land, for example, annual weeds are usually the first wild plants to appear. In succeeding years grasses gradually replace the weeds; in turn the grass is displaced by a second invasion of weeds, this time the coarse perennials such as aster and goldenrod. Young trees then gradually shade out the perennials and the land is on the way to becoming a woodland. In actuality, the successional pattern is more complex. Often most of the plant groups that seem to appear in successive invasions have been growing unnoticed in the field since its abandonment. It is only as the environment changes through time that each plant group in turn becomes dominant.

The successional route of an old field — the sequence of dominating plant species over a period of time — depends on many factors. Among these are climate, type of soil, availability of moisture, seed dispersal mechanisms of plants in the vicinity, and even the use to which the cleared land had been put. Quite often one or more of the stages mentioned above are bypassed altogether. Sometimes succession follows a fairly predictable text-

Pitch pine and Eastern red cedar, Eastham, Massachusetts. These two trees commonly invade old pastures on Cape Cod. Between the trees is a creeping mat of bearberry.

book pattern; often, however, as is true of other complex biological phenomena, the sequence seems to follow no discernible rule.

Once the field has grown to woodland, the tree community, too, will slowly change as short-lived, sun-loving pioneer species are gradually replaced by other trees. As in the case of the fast-changing old field succession, each tree species alters the environment in such a way that it can no longer grow as successfully as others. In forest succession this alteration is usually in the form of deepening shade. Most of the pioneer trees, the first to appear, cannot reproduce themselves in the deep shade. Consequently they themselves contribute to their own extinction in any one particular woodland tract.

Like old field succession, the actual pattern of succession in the forest is also complex. The same diverse factors that influence the relatively fast-moving changes in the old field also influence the varying composition of the tree community, but here discernible successional patterns are sometimes more apparent. Nevertheless, the following instances of succession are presented merely as common examples rather than as generalizations. The best way to learn about successional patterns is through careful observation in the field over a long period of time, not from reading books.

In the oak-hickory forest region of southern New England, the first trees to invade a dry field or pasture are often red cedar and gray birch. Neither tree is long-lived nor can either tolerate competition from other trees. Soon other trees begin growing in the light shade of the birches: oaks, hickories, and red maples. Within three or four decades this second generation will eliminate the cedar and birch and grow on to maturity. Where there is a bit more moisture an entirely different successional pattern may emerge.

Old field succession in northern New England. In time this pasture will probably become a coniferous forest. Balsam fir and larch are growing along the fence line; pine and spruce, in the background.

Forest succession in the sandy soil of Cape Cod and its islands is somewhat different. Red cedar usually begins the process, but within 40 years the cedar has been crowded out by a vigorous growth of pitch pine. Pitch pine, in turn, thrives for a time, but within 100 years it has almost completely given way to oaks.

In central New England and parts of the north, white pine, gray birch, and various species of shrubby cherry are the first invaders of abandoned fields. Where white pine is plentiful it often forms pure stands.

In parts of northern New England where spruce and balsam are common forest trees, it is often possible to find abandoned farmland going to pure stands of spruce, balsam, and arborvitae. In drier sites, however, birch and poplar are common pioneers. From these the forest may gradually change into the northern hardwood forest, or where the spruce was a pioneer tree it may persist as the dominant tree.

Old pasture land will almost always favor the growth of conifers. Cattle and sheep will browse on most hardwood seedlings that might appear in a pasture but they rarely eat the sour, sharp-needled conifers. To keep pasture land open, farmers periodically have had to scythe down the conifers and other inedible brush that creeps in.

In the white pine region, pasture land is often invaded by a particularly annoying shrub, the ground juniper. If not constantly controlled, within a few years this rank-growing conifer can completely choke out a pasture. But like most other old field pioneers, ground juniper is only a temporary inhabitant. Although pines usually cannot germinate under the thick branches of junipers, birch and other hardwoods can. Two decades or so later, the junipers are languishing in the shade of young hardwoods; what was once an impenetrable thicket is reduced to gnarled and twisted old trunks of dead and dying juniper.

Whether a pasture goes to pine or juniper often depends on which gets there first. A nearby pine grove, for example, usually assures the growth of pine in an old field; junipers cannot grow in the dense shade of young pine. Likewise an open pasture near a juniper thicket will probably grow to juniper rather than pine.

Forest succession is slow and complex. We have touched upon only a few of the many possible routes this process might take. Even the initial steps require decades; often a lifetime is not long enough to see the forest return to a mature climax stage.

A Place to Visit:

Phillips Andover Succession Project, Charles W. Ward Reservation, Andover, Mass. (USGS Reading & South Groveland). Route 125 at Prospect Rd. Students divided old hayfield into a number of plots which will be plowed up according to a careful schedule and then left undisturbed, allowing the vegetation to return. This is a long-term project, and visitors to the reservation in the years ahead will be able to see the stages of forest succession clearly demonstrated.

Identifying New England's Flora

Most people who enjoy the out-of-doors will probably learn to identify many of the trees and plants as a matter of course. As with other pursuits, a person's enjoyment of his natural surroundings increases in proportion to what he knows about them. In addition, being able to distinguish plants and trees raises many intriguing questions about their ecology and geography. Although New England is the most extensively botanized area in the United States, little is yet known, aside from the general limits of their ranges, about the distribution of the various species. In almost every acre of natural vegetation there exist problems of plant distribution, either for serious study or for merely a moment's reflection.

Learning to identify most of New England's flowering plants is now quite easy. Formerly it required the mastery of a cumbersome technical vocabulary and the use of complicated keys, but now there are a number of excellent non-technical manuals with color illustrations and simplified keys. Several of these are listed at the end of this section.

In addition to the guides and manuals, there are several excellent botanical gardens and plant preserves where living collections of the native flora may be observed and studied. Probably the best of these is the Will C. Curtis Garden in the Woods in Framingham, Massachusetts. The Garden in the Woods is well worth seeing anytime between the first of May and mid-October, either for a casual visit or for serious study.

The Tupper Hill reservation in Wales, Massachusetts, has another outstanding collection of native plants. It is a huge place — about 3,000 acres — and the plants are scattered throughout the preserve, wherever the habitat is most suitable. A great deal of attention has been paid to creating habitats in which the plants will survive and reproduce naturally; many species have responded by increasing their numbers. This preserve is not open for casual visits, but guided tours may be arranged in advance.

Another outstanding New England plant preserve is Bartholomew's Cobble near Ashley Falls, Massachusetts. The "Cobble" is a knob of limestone and quartzite (an acidic rock) rising out of the floor of the Housatonic River Valley. Because of its wide range of soil acidity and other conditions, this 167-acre preserve supports a large variety of plants; over 700 species have been thus far identified. A few of these have been introduced, but most are plants that were found growing naturally there. Particularly noteworthy is the large number of ferns, including several rare lime-loving species.

There are several other New England wild gardens open to the public. In Acadia National Park, near Bar Harbor, Maine, there is a small wildflower garden at Sieur de Monts Springs. There is another at historic Sturbridge Village in southern Massachusetts. The Arnold Arboretum is presently developing a wildflower preserve at its Case Estates in Weston, Massachusetts, that no doubt will prove to be a valuable addition to its many other plant collections within a few years.

The self-guiding nature trails at most of the Audubon sanctuaries and many of the state parks are also helpful to people interested in learning the native plants. Usually a booklet is available for identifying the plants and trees at various numbered stops along the trails.

Overleaf: *Bartholomew's Cobble, Ashley Falls, Massachusetts. The "cobble," a mound of limestone and quartzite, may be seen rising on the left bank of the river.*

Places to Visit:

Connecticut Arboretum, New London, Conn. Williams St. off Route 32 about .5 mile north of Route 95. Collection of native plants of the northeastern U.S. Two natural areas and wildflower garden.

The Garden in the Woods, Framingham, Mass. Route 20 to South Sudbury. South on Raymond Road to Hemenway Road. Garden entrance on left. See description in text.

Norcross Wildlife Sanctuary, Tupper Hill, Wales, Mass. (USGS Monson and Wales). South side of Monson Road about 3 miles west of Wales. See description in text. For information and appointments write Norcross Wildlife Foundation, 244 Madison Ave., New York, N.Y. 10016.

Bartholomew's Cobble, Ashley Falls, Mass. (USGS Ashley Falls). About .7 mile west of the village on the Housatonic River. See description in text.

Books to Read:

General Floras:

The New Britton and Brown Illustrated Flora by Henry Gleason (Hafner, 1963). Three large volumes, each species illustrated by line drawings. Useful to the layman but requires mastery of technical vocabulary to be of greatest value. Covers northeastern U.S. and adjacent Canada.

Gray's Manual of Botany by Merritt L. Fernald (American Book Company, 1950). The most definitive work on New England plants. Covers every known species. Knowledge of plant taxonomy a prerequisite.

Tree Guides:

Trees of North America by C. Frank Brockman and Herbert S. Zim (Golden Press, 1968). Comprehensive layman's guide to the North American trees. Excellent illustrations of each species. Non-technical descriptions and range maps.

Natural History of Trees of Eastern and Central North America by Donald Culross Peattie (Houghton Mifflin, 1950). Combination of botanical and historical facts about 150 eastern trees. Highly readable.

Master Tree Finder by May Theilgaard Watts (Nature Study Guild, 1955). Handy pocket guide to trees of the eastern and central parts of the United States. Pictured key to leaves. Shows ecology and range of trees. Well illustrated.

Tree Identification Book and *Shrub Identification Book* by George W. D. Symonds (William Morrow, 1958). Comprehensive guides to eastern trees and shrubs. Identification by photographs of leaves, fruit, bark, etc.

Trees of the Eastern and Central United States by William Harlow (Dover). Combination of identification and natural history of eastern trees.

Manual of the Trees of North America by C. S. Sargent (Dover, 1922). A two-volume condensation of Sargent's 14-volume *Silva of North America*. Line drawings. Somewhat technical.

Wildflower Guides:

Wildflowers of the United States: Volume I, The Northeastern States by Harold William Rickett (McGraw Hill, 1967). Probably the best — and most expensive — wildflower guide for the amateur. Almost all of the flowers are illustrated with full-color photographs. Volume I consists of two large volumes.

Newcombs Wildflower Guide by Lawrence Newcomb (Little, Brown, 1977). Outstanding new guide with easy-to-use key.

A Field Guide to the Wildflowers by Roger Tory Peterson (Houghton Mifflin, 1968). The long-awaited addition to the Peterson field guide series. Identifies flowers by color. Excellent for the layman.

Wild Flowers by Homer D. House (Macmillan, 1961). Large colored photographs.

Regional Guides:

New England, a Naturalist's Guide by Neil Jorgensen (Sierra Club, 1977). See description, page 146.

The Trees of New England by Lorin Dame and Henry Brooks (Dover, 1972). Reprint of 1901 edition. Some nomenclature is out of date but otherwise an excellent regional guide.

Trees and Shrubs of Northern New England by Frederic L. Steele and Albion R. Hodgdon (Society for the Protection of New Hampshire Forests, 1968). Excellent, inexpensive guide to the northern New England woody plants. Many line drawings. (Available from the Society's headquarters or from the Bookstore, University of New Hampshire, Durham, $1.60.)

Forest Trees of Southern New England (Connecticut Forest and Park Association). Pocket guide to the trees found in the southern part of the region. 75¢.

Wildflowers of Rhode Island by Irene Stuckey (University of Rhode Island, 1968). Color photographs and descriptions. (Out of Print)

Wildflowers of Connecticut by John E. Kilmas, Jr. (Walker, 1975). Color photographs and descriptions.

Wildflowers of Cape Cod by Harold Hines and Wilfred Hatheway (Chatham Press, 1968). Color photographs and descriptions. Flowers arranged by habitat. (Out of Print)

Mountain Flowers of New England. See description on page 166.

Inland Wetland Plants of Connecticut by William A. Niering and Richard H. Goodwin. See description page 178.

Fern Guides:

A Field Guide to the Ferns by Boughton Cobb (Houghton Mifflin, 1956). One of the Peterson Field Guide Series. Excellent pictured keys to aid in identification. Good for the beginner.

The Fern Guide by Edgar T. Wherry (Doubleday, 1961). More complete guide to the northeastern ferns. Slightly more advanced.

Appendixes

Maps and Aerial Photographs

Probably the most valuable single aid to learning about the landscape is the topographic map. The United States Geological Survey has mapped all of New England and published its maps in rectangular sections called *quadrangles*. The actual area covered in a quadrangle varies. In southern New England each quadrangle covers an area of about 6 by 8 miles at a scale of 1 inch on the map equaling about 2,000 feet on the ground; farther north the maps are of a smaller scale, each quadrangle covering an area of about 12 by 16 miles at a scale of about 1 inch equaling 1 mile. The maps are of a convenient size, small enough to be spread out on a desk or folded compactly to fit in a pocket.

These topographic maps, printed in five colors, contain a wealth of information. Roads, trails, railroads, boundaries, houses, and other man-made features are printed in black. Water features — lakes, rivers, swamps, and waterfalls — are printed in blue. Principal highways are printed in red. Woodlands, if shown, are represented by a green overprint. Contour lines indicating the elevation and shape of the terrain are printed in brown. Contour lines are probably the best way to represent accurately the ups and downs of the terrain on a flat surface. It takes practice and imagination to visualize hills and valleys from the contours on the map but, once mastered, this ability increases manyfold the usefulness of the map. A free booklet explaining the symbols used on topographic maps may be obtained from the Geological Survey.

People who enjoy the out-of-doors find these maps useful in many ways. Back roads, hiking trails, landmarks, and local points of interest are all clearly shown. If a person wishes to take to the woods he can easily avoid houses and fields by traveling only in the areas shown by green overprinting. Obstructions such as swamps, cliffs, and wide rivers are easily avoided. A hiker equipped with a compass and a topographic map of the region he is traversing would

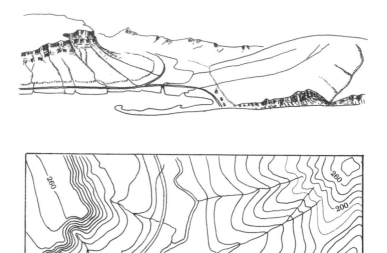

Contour Interval 20 ft.

The upper drawing is a view of a river valley between two hills. The hill on the right is gently sloping whereas the one on the left forms a series of cliffs. The river flows into a bay which is partially enclosed by a hooked sandbar. These same features are shown on the topographic map below. The actual form of the land in the upper drawing is represented on the map by contour lines.

find it difficult to become lost — provided, of course, he knows how to use both.

As a person becomes familiar with the use of these maps, he becomes able to visualize the terrain even without seeing it. We have already noted in the text that such surface features as eskers, drumlins, and kettleholes may be directly read from the topographic maps; with practice other features may be identified as well.

In addition to these large-scale maps, the Geological Survey publishes another series of topographic maps at a smaller scale. Each of these maps covers a much larger area, about 60 by 100 miles, at a scale of 1 inch to 4 miles. Although they are correspondingly less detailed, these maps, because they cover a much larger area, are useful for planning trips and getting an overall impression of the terrain. Recently the Army Map Service has printed these small-scale maps on moulded plastic sheets that actually give a three-dimensional picture of the terrain. The vertical scale has been exaggerated several times so that even small hills and valleys are clearly seen.

Both the large- and small-scale topographic maps may be purchased from the Geological Survey in Washington, D.C., or, at a slightly higher price, from many commercial agents such as sporting goods stores, bookstores, or news agencies. Each quadrangle is named, usually for a principal city or prominent landmark located within the area of the map. Index maps for each state showing the quadrangles as well as the areas covered by the small-scale series in red overprint are available from the Geological Survey without charge. The three-dimensional maps may be ordered from Hubbard Scientific Company, Northbrook, Illinois, 60062

Topographic maps of various mountain areas in New England, showing hiking trails in more detail than do the Geological Survey maps, are published by the Appalachian Mountain Club. These trail maps are regularly revised to keep them up to date.

The geology of many of the quadrangles has also been mapped. Massachusetts, Connecticut, and Rhode Island are engaged in a cooperative program of mapping with the U.S. Government. Geologic quadrangle maps of Maine, New Hampshire, and Vermont are available through the state agencies listed in the appendix. The coverage of these large-scale geological maps is not complete. Lists of those quadrangles mapped and published thus far is available from the Geological Survey or from the various states that are doing their own surveying. The usual practice is to show the bedrock geology and the surficial geology on separate maps; most maps are accompanied by a description of the geology. Although these maps are most useful to people with some background in geology, they do contain a great deal of information that is understandable by the amateur. Especially useful are the maps showing the surficial geology, the glacial and other surface features that are easy to observe and comprehend.

In addition, the federal government maintains a complete file of aerial photographs of New England. These may be ordered covering various sized areas and at various enlargements. The Map Information Office of the U.S. Geological Survey can supply price lists and the serial numbers for the aerial photographs desired from a description of the area to be covered.

Mailing Addresses

Below are listed complete mailing addresses for government and private agencies that publish information on New England's geology, scenery, and plant geography.

U.S. Government Agencies:

For topographic and geologic maps:
U.S. Geological Survey
Washington, D.C., 20242
Free index of topographic maps available for each of the New England States.

For information about aerial photographs:
Map Information Office
U.S. Geological Survey
Washington, D.C., 20242

For U.S. geologic publications other than maps:
Superintendent of Documents
U.S. Government Printing Office
Washington, D.C., 20402

State Agencies:

Connecticut geological and natural history publications may be ordered from:
Department of Environmental Protection
Natural Resources Center
State Office Building
Hartford, Connecticut, 06106
Free list of publications. Connecticut residents add 8% sales tax.

Maine geological publications may be ordered from:
Maine Geological Survey
State House Station #22
Augusta, Maine, 04333
Free list of publications. Checks made payable to the Treasurer of the State of Maine. Maine residents add 5% sales tax.

New Hampshire geological publications may be ordered from:
New Hampshire Department Economic Development
P.O. Box 856
Concord, New Hampshire, 03301
Free list of publications.

Vermont geological publications may be ordered from:
Vermont State Library
c/o State Office Building Post Office
Montpelier, Vermont, 05602
Free list of publications.

Private Non-profit Organizations:

Appalachian Mountain Club
5 Joy Street
Boston, Massachusetts, 02108
Free list of publications and club information. Mass. residents add 5% sales tax.

Connecticut Audubon Society
2325 Burr Street
Fairfield, Connecticut, 06430
Conn. residents add 8% sales tax.

Connecticut Forest and Park Association
16 Meriden Road — Route 66
Middletown, Connecticut, 06457
Conn. residents add 8% sales tax.

Massachusetts Audubon Society
South Great Road
Lincoln, Massachusetts, 01773

The Nature Conservancy
2093 K Street, N.W.
Washington, D.C., 20005

New England Wildflower Society
Hemenway Road
Framingham, Massachusetts 01701
Free list of publications. Mass. residents add 5% sales tax.

Society for the Protection of New Hampshire Forests
5 South State Street
Concord, New Hampshire, 03301

The Trustees of Reservations
224 Adams Street
Milton, Massachusetts, 02108
Free brochure on Massachusetts natural areas and historic sites owned by the Trustees.

Glossary

Alluvial fan A deposit of sand and gravel made by a stream where it runs out onto a level plain, so called because of its shape.

Basalt A fine-grained, dark-colored igneous rock formed by the solidification of lava. The hills in the Connecticut Valley are mainly basalt.

Boulder train A fan-shaped scattering of boulders and rocks which originated from a single bedrock knob and were carried to their resting place by glacial ice. The boulders lie intermingled with other rock types in the glacial debris. The significance of boulder trains is that they show the general direction of glacial movement.

Cirque A deep steep-walled hollow in a mountainside formed by glacial erosion. Tuckerman's and Huntington Ravines are cirques on Mt. Washington.

Conglomerate A sedimentary rock containing rounded, water-worn rock fragments cemented together by another mineral substance.

Coniferous forest A forest consisting chiefly of cone-bearing trees with needle-shaped leaves.

Deciduous forest A forest consisting chiefly of trees that lose their leaves during some season of the year, usually in autumn. Deciduous forests are also known as hardwood forests.

Dike A sheet-like body of igneous rock that cuts across the structure of adjacent rocks, usually formed when molten rock material from the interior of the earth has forced its way toward the surface through a wide crack.

Drumlin A hill of glacial till usually shaped like an inverted teaspoon, with the long axis lying parallel to the direction of the flow of glacial ice. Most drumlins are less than 200 feet high and a mile long.

Esker A long, narrow ridge of sand and gravel which probably was once the bed of a stream in or beneath the ice of a glacier and was left behind when the ice melted. Some of the world's longest eskers occur in eastern Maine.

Fault A crack in the earth's crust along which movement has taken place so that the rock strata on either side no longer match.

Glacial erratic A boulder that has been transported from its source by glacial ice, sometimes over a considerable distance, and then left stranded when the ice melted. Glacial erratics are usually of a different rock type than the bedrock on which they lie.

Gneiss A type of metamorphic rock with a banded structure. The banding is due to the separation of light and dark minerals by heat and pressure. Gneiss is a common rock across much of New England.

Granite A coarse-grained igneous rock containing quartz, feldspar, and other minerals. Its structure is coarse enough so that the individual mineral grains can be clearly distinguished. It is usually a very hard and durable rock, and one that is quite common across much of New England.

Igneous rock Rock that has solidified from a molten state, either within the earth or on the surface. Basalt and granite are examples.

Joint A crack in the bedrock along which no appreciable movement occurred. Most of New England's granite shows distinct jointing.

Kame terrace A flattish body of sand and gravel deposited by running water between a stagnant lobe of glacial ice and an adjacent valley wall. Many of Vermont's valleys have kame terraces along their margins.

Kettlehole A bowl-shaped depression formed as a result of a large mass of ice becoming detached from the melting glacier and being buried by gravel from meltwater streams. As the ice block subsequently melts the depression is formed.

Krummholz Dense, stunted trees growing near the timber line on high mountains. The height of the trees usually corresponds to the depth of the winter snow cover; new summer growth that extends above the snow is usually killed back by the severe winter weather.

Lee slope The side of a hill that faces away from the direction from which the glacial ice came. In New England the lee slopes of hills are usually steep.

Mantle rock The layer of loose rock material that lies on top of the solid bedrock. The surface layer of the mantle rock is usually soil. Nearly all of New England's mantle rock has been deposited by glaciers.

Metamorphic rock Rock which was originally igneous or sedimentary that has been changed in character and appearance, usually by heat and pressure. Sometimes the process of metamorphosis changes rock so greatly that its original form is impossible to determine. The majority of New England's rock is metamorphic.

Monadnock An isolated hill or mountain that stands above the surrounding area because its rock has been more resistant to erosion. Monadnocks are named after New Hampshire's Mt. Monadnock, which was formed in this way.

Moraine Rock material deposited directly by a glacier and left in piles that are independent of the underlying bedrock topography. A *terminal* or *end moraine* is formed at the most advanced end of a glacier when debris being carried by the glacier is piled up into a line of low hills.

Outwash plain A sandy or gravelly plain consisting of glacial debris formed by streams originating from the melting ice of a glacier. Much of Cape Cod and the adjacent islands are outwash plains.

Peneplain A land surface worn down by erosion to a nearly flat or broadly undulating plain, or such a surface uplifted to form a plateau and subjected to renewed erosion. Much of southern New England is thought to be an uplifted peneplain.

Plutonic rock Igneous rock that has solidified deep within the earth. Plutonic rocks have cooled slowly and are thus characterized by relatively large crystals of their constituent minerals. Granite is a good example of plutonic rock.

Podzol A soil formed in a cool and moist climate that is characterized by a leached, grayish-white layer. Podzols are found mainly in regions of coniferous forests.

Quartzite A hard, granular metamorphic rock derived from sandstone.

Residual soil Soil formed *in situ* by the disintegration and decomposition of the underlying bedrock. Because of the scraping action of the glacial ice, residual soil is rare in New England.

Rock flour Finely ground rock particles resulting from glacial abrasion.

Scarp A cliff or steep slope.

Schist A medium or coarse-grained metamorphic rock with more or less parallel orientation of the micaceous minerals. Schists, common across much of New England, usually can be broken into thin plates.

Sedimentary rock Rock which has been formed from materials that have been transported by wind, water, or ice. Sedimentary rocks are usually layered.

Sheet joints Joints in bedrock that are essentially parallel to the surface of the ground. Sheet joints are closely spaced near the surface and become progressively farther apart with increasing depth. They are especially well developed in granitic rocks.

Sphagnum A coarse, soft moss found chiefly on the surface of bogs; also called peat moss.

Stagnation zone An area of a glacier, usually near its terminus, where the ice is too thin to move.

Stoss slope The slope of a hill facing the direction from which the glacier has moved.

Talus A pile of boulders and broken rock of all sizes which accumulates at the foot of a cliff.

Tannin An acidic vegetable compound found especially in oak trees.

Terminal moraine See Moraine.

Thrust fault A low-angle fault in which the upper side rides over the lower side. Thrust faults have had a great effect upon the geology of western Vermont.

Till The layer of rocks and rock particles of many sizes that have been dragged along in the lower part of a glacier and left behind when the ice melted. Till is often a tough, unstratified clay loaded with different-sized rocks.

Tillite A sedimentary rock composed of cemented till.

Varve A pair of sediments consisting of a lower coarse layer, usually silt, and an upper fine layer, usually clay, deposited in a lake from inflowing streams.

Volcanic ash Fine particles of lava that have been ejected from a volcano during eruption.

Volcanic bomb A lump of lava which has been ejected from a volcano and assumes a rounded shape as it flies through the air.

Index

252

Pegmatite, 67–76, *68*
Peneplain, 20–21, 22–23, 24, 26, 28, *50*
Penwood State Park (Conn.), 59
Perry Woods, 183
Peterborough, N.H., 24
Petersham, Mass., 205
Phillips Andover Succession Project (Mass.), 233
Phillipston, Mass., 220
Pine: pitch, 203, 222–24, *223, 229;* white, *139,* 179, 188, 190, 191–95
Pine River, N.H., 123, 125
Pinkham Notch (N.H.), 88, 95
Pisgah Tract (N.H.), *185,* 188, *189,* 194
Pitcher plant, 171, *172*
Pittsburg, N.H., 154, 155
Plainfield, N.H., 183
Plainfield Hardwood Slope (N.H.), 183
Platt Hill Park (Conn.), 221
Plutonic rock, 42, 45
Plymouth, Mass., 116
Pocumtuck Hills (Mass.), 53
Podzol, 153, 181, 223, 224
Poison ivy, 213
Poison sumac, 175
Pomperaug Valley (Conn.), 51, 52
Portland, Conn., 73, 75
Portland, Me., *135*
Presidential Range, 42, 91, 96; alpine zone, *156*–57, 158, 161, *162,* 164, 165–66
Primeval hardwood forest, 184–90, *185*
Princeton, Mass., 24, 77
Proctor, Vt., 35, 36, 37
Purple loosestrife, 214

Quartz, *41,* 67, 68, 72, 153
Quartzite, 30, 235

Rhododendron, 216, 217–18, 220, 225–27
Rhododendron State Park (N.H.), 217, 220
Rhodora, 171, 217
Rice Mine (N.H.), 72, 75
Rock flour, 87
Rocking stones, 102
Rocky Hill, Conn., 56, 60, 129, 131
Route 2, Mass., 29, 30, 57, 60
Route 3, Mass., 137
Route 6, Mass., 114
Route 7, Vt., 32, 35

Route 16, N.H., 123, 125
Route 22A, Vt., 37
Route 100, Vt., 30
Roxbury, Conn., 63
Ruggles Mine (N.H.), 72, 75
Rumford, Me., 64, 71, 72, 74
Rye, N.H., 138

Saddleback Mountain (Me.), 166
Sagamore, Mass., 114
St. Johnsbury, Vt., 118, 129, 131
St. Lawrence Valley, 84, 130, *133*
Sandstone, 48, *50,* 52, 54, 58, 59
Sandwich, Mass., 114, 115, 226, 227
Sandwich Moraine (Mass.), 114
Sawyer Rock (N.H.), 103
Schist, 40, 66
Sea level changes, 132–38, *133, 135*
Shade Swamp Sanctuary (Conn.), 177
Shale, 48, *50,* 52, 54, *55,* 57, 58
Shelburne, Vt., 37, 118
Shoot Flying Hill (Mass.), 222
Sieur de Monts Springs (Me.), 235
Silver, 63
Skinner State Park (Mass.), 59
Slate, 37
Sleeping Giant State Park (Conn.), 206
Smith's Ferry, Mass., 56, 60
Soucook River (N.H.), 125
South Hadley, Mass., 56
South Moat Mountain (N.H.), 44
Southwest Harbor, Me., 177
Sphagnum, 170, 171, 173, 175
Springvale, Me., 217, 220
Spruce, 149, 179; bog, *169,* 173, *174,* 176, 177; spruce-fir forest, 147–55, *148*
Stagnation zone, 116
Stonington, Conn., 203–4
Stoss and lee topography, *86, 87,* 91
Stowe, Vt., 30
Stratton Mountain (Vt.), 28
Strickland Quarry (Conn.), 73, 75
Sturbridge Village, Mass., 235
Succession: bog, *169,* 170–73, *174,* 176, 177; forest, 230,